MISERY AND MISFORTUNE
SUDDEN DEATHS IN SUFFOLK
1800-1850

Geoffrey Robinson

Other books by the Author
Worlingworths Fallen 1914-1918
Worlingworth Past and Present In Photographs Vols 1 & 2

The author wishes to acknowledge the assistance
of Suffolk Local History Council via the
Gwen Dyke Fund in the publication of this book.

Researched, written, and published by Geoffrey Robinson.

ISBN 978-0-9572292-3-5

Printed in Great Britain by The Lavenham Press Limited.
First published in 2017
Copyright Geoffrey Robinson 2017

Front Cover: Wilby church and poor cottages (early 19th century engraving)
Back Cover: Worlingworth church (as depicted in Monograph of St. Mary's
Church Worlingworth by David Ross CIE)

CONTENTS

LIST OF ILLUSTRATIONS

INTRODUCTION

Life was a continuous struggle for the families of the working classes in Suffolk who lived during the first half of the nineteenth century. Surviving your infancy and childhood was a feat in itself when infectious diseases and malnutrition threatened your very existence. Working from the age of 12 or 14 in a labour-intensive occupation under difficult conditions was never likely to lead to a comfortable old age. The prospect of a harsh winter meant that many, both old and young, suffered terribly from the cold with only the flickering embers of the hearth to huddle round.

And yet the 19th century saw many transformations in people's lives, not least in their health and life expectancy. People's health improved and average life expectancy increased. In the first half of the nineteenth century, the population of Suffolk rose from 214,404 in 1801 to 337,215 in 1851. This increase occurred because of a rapidly increasing birth rate and a declining death rate. This was despite the number of deaths that were incurred by tuberculosis, cholera and other infectious diseases.

Deaths in infancy and through senile decay contributed a large share towards the mortality statistics for the county. In amongst those large numbers were deaths attributable to hazards in the household and those deaths that occurred due to the misfortune of the deceased. An increasing feature of the provincial newspapers was the reporting of these sudden deaths.

The Ipswich Journal and the Bury & Norwich Post were the principal provincial newspapers of Suffolk during the first half of the 19th century. The Ipswich Journal (used as the primary source in this book) was established in 1720 and was published weekly. Its pages were initially filled with advertising and national news, but as this and other newspapers developed, the content became increasingly devoted to local news and in particular to local news that concerned death.

It was death, whether it was from murder, suicide or just accidental death that sold newspapers and titillated and shocked their middle-class readership in the early 19th century. From grisly tales of murder in the backstreets of a metropolitan slum to the incredible loss of life from the sinking of some unsinkable leviathan on the high seas, death and the explanation for it captivated the print-reading masses. In many instances, it was what one could only describe as the banality of death which fascinated those readers. By this we mean how, from very ordinary circumstances, someone could be snatched by the jaws of death from the meagre poverty of their existence.

The Ipswich Journal was a very good example of a provincial newspaper which provided its readership with that fascinating experience. Violence and death (in particular, violent death) became a continual and predominant feature of its weekly output, covering local disasters, fires, accidents and criminal proceedings and most of all, in the reporting of coroners inquests. As the first half of the 19th century wore on, the reporting of inquest proceedings increased in number and in the detail reported.

In this book, we will examine the proceedings of a coroner's inquest with particular reference to a rural inquest; an event that rivalled the auction, the communal harvest home, the hunt or the cart colt show in enlivening the sometimes dreary existence of the inhabitants.

We will look at a typical coroner's inquest in detail using an example drawn from the very extensive archives of the Suffolk Record Office. Finally for the bulk of the text, we will take a chronological journey through the pages of the Ipswich Journal from 1800 to 1850 to read about some of the reports of sudden deaths and the inquests resulting from those deaths. Interspersed with the text you will find some old photographic images of inns and taverns that may have been the settings for coroners inquests in the past. Most of these old buildings that closed their doors to the thirsty labourer many years ago can still be located in our Suffolk parishes today.

It seems unimaginable in our safety-conscious environment today that so many of the sudden deaths described within the pages of this book could happen, and happen repeatedly. Stories of negligence, stupidity and oft-times just sheer bad luck provide us with a view into a world where death walked behind you and life seemed almost valueless. Of course, what the newspaper reports and this book cannot describe is the unimaginable anguish that bereaved families endured, knowing, as they did, in what bizarre or lamentable way their loved ones had perished.

My interest in this aspect of life in the nineteenth century stems from extensive research into the local history of my own parish - Worlingworth - and a fascination with the seemingly ordinary headstones and their inscriptions in the churchyard. Every headstone inscription has a story to tell - in most cases, stories of indescribable sadness. The tales of sudden death described in this book and the misery and misfortune that endured offer us a peep-hole into a vulnerable society far removed from our own today.

Virtually all of the reports of sudden deaths that have been used in this book have been drawn from the pages of the Ipswich Journal. In order to maintain some brevity, individual references to each of these newspaper articles are not given as an appendix. Archive newspaper websites and microfilm at the Suffolk Record Office have provided this source material, which remains available to the interested researcher. Any mistakes or omissions in the text and indexes are entirely the fault of the author.

Geoffrey Robinson
December 2017

1

The Coroner's Inquest in a Rural Setting

The rural Coroner's Court, where inquests took place, was a public space where bystanders and reporters jostled with jurors, relatives and witnesses for breathing space in the confines of, for example, the local inn or schoolroom. Sensational details of the death that had occurred would be hastily recorded by the reporter and rushed into newsprint, the column space being given for such an inquest being directly related to its sensationalism. Violent accidental deaths were accorded the most detailed coverage, especially when the victim was a child. In competition with an unusual suicide or the tragic death of a child, the reporting of a church harvest festival or village fete paled into insignificance.

The work of the County Coroner is worth describing in some detail. Since the end of the 12th century, the coroner's role in England has been to investigate sudden and suspicious deaths that occurred within their jurisdiction.

The County Coroner was elected by a body of freeholders and he would be expected to be in post for life, combining the duties of the post with his other work. There were originally no qualification requirements for the post of coroner; surprisingly, knowledge of medical matters was not necessary. Instead, according to the Coroners Act of 1887, the chief requisites were discretion, tact, common sense, perception, sympathy and a knowledge of human nature.

Despite the fact that no legal or medical qualifications were required, great care was often taken to appoint a suitable person; in fact, like the coroners of today, many Victorian coroners were trained solicitors.

A coroner's work might only take up a few hours each week but the work sometimes involved extensive travel around the county. Inquests were normally held within 48 hours of the person's death or of the body being discovered and the venue in a rural parish was most likely to be the public house or village inn.

The jury would be comprised of at least twelve local men and these were generally tradesmen, shopkeepers and artisans rather than the working class labourers. There were no statutory qualifications required for serving as a juror and in the smaller parishes, it would not have been uncommon for the jurymen to know the deceased and the witnesses brought before them.

The inquest started once the jury, witnesses, any press reporters and interested members of the public had crammed themselves into the room that would host the formal proceedings. The body of the deceased might already have been placed on a table in the room so that the Coroner and jurymen could view it. In the case of a burns victim, the shocking state of the scorched cadaver must have presented a most horrible sight to those assembled.

Once a brief visual examination of the body had been completed by the Coroner and jury, it would probably be returned to its temporary place of rest (which would most likely have been the coolest place in the building, possibly upstairs on the landing under the floorboards).

The Coroner's Inquest - Bring the body in!

Witness testimonies would then be heard by the Court. Much of the questioning of witnesses was done by the Coroner, though jurors could interject with their own questions and they frequently did. Character witnesses might be called in cases where children had fallen victim to an accident in the home, when the mother's ability to care for the child might be called into question.

The Coroner frequently called upon medical witnesses to give evidence and medical practitioners would be asked to give their account of any medical treatment they had provided and also their opinion into the cause of death. The power to summon a medical witness was passed into law in 1836. A medical examination of the body usually amounted to a perfunctory external examination. A post-mortem examination was still a relatively infrequent occurrence.

After hearing all the witness statements, the Coroner would sum up the evidence in his address to the jury and they would then give their verdict. The Coroner might give the jury some direction in how they might reach a particular verdict but the verdict of the Coroner's inquest was the sole responsibility of the jury.

Once the verdict had been given, the inquest was over and many of the participants would return to their homes. Perhaps if the inquest was held in the local hostelry, the landlord would provide refreshment for the Coroner and the jury in the form of a cold collation. There would undoubtedly be much discussion over the circumstances of the sudden death amongst the regulars. It would be the talk of the parish for some time afterwards.

The press reporters would return to their offices as soon as possible and begin to write their report on the inquest proceedings for the next edition of their newspaper. Both the Coroner and the members of the press corps might have a number of inquests to attend over a short period of time; it might not have been very comfortable, during a severe winter, travelling from one remote parish to the next on uneven roads in all weathers. Nevertheless, it had to be done.

Inquest proceedings were scrupulously recorded. A complete record of each inquest with all of its accompanying documentation (written witness statements, etc) would be kept. A typical example of the documentary record of an inquest, held by the Suffolk Records Office, is reproduced in the next chapter.

2

Inquest on the body of Elizabeth Leech

The documentation that recorded the proceedings of the inquest was meticulously prepared, written and archived - many of these original documents still exist and are kept in excellent condition by the Suffolk Record Office. I examined one such record concerning the inquest into the death of a small child, Elizabeth Leech, who was killed when a hearse ran over her close to the parish boundary between Earl Soham and Bedfield. The inquest took place at the Falcon Inn, Earl Soham on Wednesday 16th September 1801.

On the preceding day, the Constable for the parish of Earl Soham received a printed message from the Coroner, John Wood, Gent., which said: *"These are in his Majesty's Name, to require and command you, on Sight hereof to summons and warn four and twenty good and lawful Men of Discretion and Understanding, living within four or more Parishes near adjoining to the said Parish of Earl Soham, personally to be and appear before me, his Majesty's Coroner for the said Liberty at the House of the Widow Black, known by the Name or Sign of the Falcon in Earl Soham aforesaid, on Wednesday the sixteenth Day of September by four of the Clock in the afternoon of the same Day; then and there to serve on a Jury, to enquire of all such Matters and Things as shall be given them in Charge and in particular, how, and in what Manner Elizabeth Leech, an infant of the age of six years lately deceased, came by her Death. And you are hereby required to be then and there present, to make Return hereof, and also to give*

personal Notice to all Persons that can give any Evidence concerning the affair, that they may also attend. And hereof you are not to fail, as you will answer it at your several Perils."
Given under my Hand and Seal of Office, this 15th Day of September in the Year of our Lord 1801. John Wood, Coroner.
(Author's italics)

A list of the names of the men chosen to serve on the Jury accompanied the witness statements. The witness statements then went as follows:
An Examination of Witnesses Sworn and Examined at the Parish of Earl Soham in the Liberty of Saint Etheldred in the County of Suffolk on the Sixteenth Day of September in the Year of our Lord One Thousand Eight Hundred and One before John Wood, Gentleman, Coroner of the said Liberty, on view of the body of Elizabeth Leech, an Infant of the age six years or thereabouts then and there lying dead.

Hannah Leech, the wife of Thomas Leech of Earl Soham, Laborer, upon her oath, saith that about half after two o'clock on Monday the 14th of September instant, her daughter Elizabeth seeing a hearse with a pair of horses travelling in the open road in the parish of Earl Soham aforesaid, ran after it for the purpose of opening a gate about a quarter of a mile off in the parish of Bedfield, that about a quarter of an hour after, two young children informed her that her daughter was dead, that she was killed with the hearse going over her, upon which the Examinant immediately ran to the gate and found the deceased laying upon the ground in the road quite dead.

The Falcon Inn, Earl Soham

James Ashford of Brundish in the County of Suffolk, husbandman, upon his oath saith that between the hours of 2 and 3 on Monday afternoon last he was driving a hearse with a pair of horses in the open high road in the parish of Bedfield and passing through a gate standing across the road, he saw the deceased and two other children standing on the before part of the gate, holding it open for the hearse to go through, that this Examinant threw them a halfpenny for opening the gate, that he passed through the gate without stopping or saying anything to either of the children, and that he did not in passing this or afterwards hear any of them cry out, nor did he know that any accident had happened to any of them till about 3 in the afternoon of the next day Tuesday - when he was told of it by Mr. John Ludbrook, who was upon the Jury.

Phoebe Harvey, a child about 8 years of age and daughter of Robert Harvey of Earl Soham, husbandman, saith that on

Monday afternoon between 2 and 3, she was playing with the deceased in the open road in the parish of Bedfield, that a hearse with two horses was passing that way, that she together with the deceased and another younger child all ran to open a gate, which was standing across the road, that the driver in going through the gate, threw down a halfpenny for them and that the deceased, eager to get it, threw herself down upon the ground to scramble for it, and that the hind wheel on the right side went against her head - that the deceased did not call out or make any noise at all, nor yet struggle, but died instantly, and that the other little girl lifted her up and found her quite dead, and this examinant then ran and told the deceased's mother of the accident.

The Jury's verdict stated "that the said Elizabeth Leech, on the fourteenth day of September in the year aforesaid, being in the Common Road or Kings Highway in the parish of Bedfield in the County of Suffolk and Liberty aforesaid with two other small children and in endeavouring to pick up a halfpenny thrown to them by James Ashford, who was driving a common hearse with two horses in the said Common Road, that the said Elizabeth Leech fell down and that the off hind wheel of the said hearse by accident went against her head by means whereof she received a violent wound or contusion upon her forehead of which said wound or contusion she there and then instantly died, and so the Jurors aforesaid, upon their oath, say that the said Elizabeth Leech came to her death by accident in manner aforesaid and not otherwise. And further the Jurors aforesaid do say that the said hearse and wheels thereof moved to the death of the said Elizabeth Leech and are now in the possession of William Smith of Helmingham, the proprietor thereof and are of the value of five shillings." In Witness thereof (signed by the Jurors).

The 'deodand' of five shillings needs some explanation. The term 'deodand' derives from the Latin phrase 'deo dandum', which means 'to be given to God'. In law, a deodand was a thing which was given to God; specifically it was an object or animal which became forfeit because it had caused a person's death. In theory, the deodand was forfeit to the Crown, which was supposed to sell the object or animal and use the profits for pious use. In reality the coroner's juries, who decided that a particular object or animal was a deodand, also appraised its value and the owner or owners were expected to pay a fine equal to the value of the deodand. If they could not pay the deodand, the parish was held responsible. So in the case of Elizabeth Leech, it was William Smith, the owner of the hearse and its wheels, who had to pay five shillings 'deodand'.

A further illustration of the form that a deodand took is given in a coroner's inquest, held in November 1803, some details of which were as follows:

Inquisition on the death of Henry Durrant at Monewden, Nov. 6 1803 - killed inside of a mill.

An Inquisition indented, taken on the behalf of our Sovereign Lord the King, at the Parish of Monewden in the Liberty of Saint Etheldred, in the County of Suffolk, on the sixth day of November in the forty fourth year of the Reign of our Sovereign Lord George the third by the Grace of God of the United Kingdom of Great Britain and Ireland, King, Defender of the Faith. And in the year of our Lord One thousand eight Hundred and three.

Before JOHN WOOD, Gentleman, Coroner of the said Liberty, on view of the body of Henry Durrant, then and there lying dead, upon the oath of Peter Kersey, Peter Sparke, Henry Canter, John Wright, Edward Adams, James Garnham, Benjamin Ludbrook, Charles Ashford, William Kitson, Christopher Woods, John Jenners, John Marjoram, Samuel Gall, Robert Harvey and William Pitts, good and lawful Men of the Liberty aforesaid then and there Sworn and Charged to inquire for our said Lord the King, when, where, how, and in what manner the said Henry Durrant came to his Death, who upon their Oath say,

That the said Henry Durrant on the fifth day of November in the year aforesaid, being at work in a windmill of James Durrant in Monewden aforesaid in the Liberty aforesaid in the County aforesaid and being near to the cogs of the wheel of the said windmill, the said cogs by accident caught hold of him the said Henry Durrant by which means he received several mortal wounds and bruises upon his head and other parts of his body of which and mortal wound and bruises he then and there on the said mill died.

And as the Jurors aforesaid upon their oath say that the said Henry Durrant came to his death by accident in manner aforesaid and not otherwise. And further the Jurors aforesaid do say that this said wheel and cogs thereof moved to the death of the said Henry Durrant and are in the possession of James Durrant of Monewden aforesaid miller and are of the value of four shillings.

In Witness whereof as well, the said Coroner as the Jurors aforesaid have to this inquisition set their hands and seals the day year and place first above written. (Author's italics)

So the deodand to be paid in this instance was four shillings, equivalent to half of a labourer's weekly wage.

It should also be noted that the expenses of the coroner were written down and recorded as follows:

Inquisition £1-0-0; 10 miles   7s-6d

The coroner was not paid a salary but he was able to claim travelling expenses and he was also paid a sum for each inquest he presided over.

3

Sudden Deaths and Inquests 1800-1820

We shall now learn of some of the different ways by which men and women met their end in the first two decades of the 19th century. Many of these inquest documents are carefully preserved and looked after by the Suffolk Record Office for which we are very grateful. These records are far too numerous to reproduce in this book and a selection is brought to the reader's attention.

Many of these sudden deaths, or the inquests that followed, were reported with increasing frequency in the columns of the Ipswich Journal. During the period covered by this chapter, reporting in newspapers was brief. The coroner's inquest documents have been studied in order to give the reader a better appreciation of some of the more unusual cases.

Our journey begins with the summary of an inquest into the death of Margaret Mills, the wife of a labourer. The inquest took place on October 13th 1800. The distressing event that led to the inquest took place in the parish of Kenton and the inquest was convened in the parish church. This was an unusual place to hold the inquest. In the course of researching this book, no other instances of a church being used have been discovered. It can only be presumed that the local inn, the Kenton Crown, and the school were not available. John Wood, the Coroner for the Liberty of St. Etheldred, presided and the facts elucidated were as follows.

The husband Edmund Mills and a lodger John Hill testified under oath that the woman had been in a melancholy state of mind for a number of years and her mental state had progressively worsened. On the morning of the 13th, after a largely sleepless night, the deceased rose and went out of the house. When her husband rose about half an hour later, the deceased had not returned and he went out looking for his wife. She was found by the husband floating face down in a pond which was located in a meadow known as the Priory Field. The husband on discovering his wife's body called for some assistance which duly arrived and the body was recovered from the pond.

The lodger, John Mills, also testified to the same facts and the jury, made up of fifteen local men, gave their verdict that the deceased, Margaret Mills, being a lunatic and not of sound mind, did go alone to the pond and did then and there voluntarily cast and throw herself into the said pond of water by means whereof she was then and there immediately suffocated and drowned.

There were fifteen named jurors all of whom had to sign their names to the document which detailed the verdict. Four of those men were unable to sign their names and therefore gave their mark. The Coroner, John Wood Esq. was paid one pound for the inquest and thirteen shillings and sixpence for the ten miles that he travelled back and forth to Kenton. The body of Margaret Mills would have been buried at the roadside, not in the consecrated ground of the churchyard.

Death by misadventure is a term used as a verdict in present-day inquests and it could have been applied to the tragic occurrence that took place in Eyke in February 1801.

John Wood, Gent., the Coroner, investigated the sudden death of James Fisk, a twelve year old boy who drowned in a pond. John Sherwood, a farmer, gave evidence although he was not the principal witness. He spoke on behalf of Mary Jolly, who came to him at about 4 o'clock on the afternoon of February 18th, telling him that one of Master Fisk's children had fallen into the pond and she was afraid that he had drowned. She said it was James Fisk and Sherwood immediately went to the pond with other persons where they took the young boy out of the water. There was no sign of life. Sherwood then stated that he believed that Fisk, being at play with several other children on the ice of the frozen pond, had fallen into the pond as the ice broke. The boy was immediately suffocated and drowned. This "hearsay" evidence was sufficient for the jury to return the verdict that the boy had drowned accidentally.

A remarkable case occurred at Friston in August 1804 on the death of an infant, Mary Mills, of the age of one year or thereabouts. Once again John Wood, Gent., was the presiding coroner. The case which involved a game cock was distressing in its detail and therefore only the written verdict is reproduced.

That the said Mary Mills, being at play in the road near to the yard of John Mills, her father, in Friston aforesaid, and a game cock being near there, the said game cock by accident got to the said child and seized upon her and picked and clawed her about the head and face in a shocking manner by which means she received divers wounds and bruises on her head and face, of which said wounds and bruises she languished for five weeks until the sixth day of August and then died.

The offending game cock was subsequently killed.

A week later, coroner John Wood, Gent., was required to hold an inquest at Earl Soham on the body of Edward Peck, an infant of the age of two years or thereabouts. The inquest took place in the house of the parents, Benjamin and Elizabeth Peck. The jury consisted of fifteen local men. A summation of the evidence is given here.

> The wife, on her oath, said that on Saturday 11th August at about half past nine in the morning, her infant babe came into the house and had something to drink and went out into the yard again. She said that about half an hour after, another of the children, James, about four years old, came in and said "Mother, Edward is drowned" and she said "Where, dear?" and the child said "In Mr. Clubbe's water." The examinant immediately went to the spot and jumped into the water, and called out very much for help. Sometime afterwards, a neighbour came and pulled out the examinant, she being not able to get her child out. She said that about seven or eight minutes afterwards, the child was taken out of the water but there appeared no signs of life in it. She believed from what her infant son

James told her that the child, by accident, slipped under the rail into the water and was drowned. The jury returned a verdict accordingly.

A curious incident occurred in the centre of Ipswich in August 1805 and was reported in the Ipswich Journal:

An inquisition was held before W. Norris and S. Jackaman, Gents., Coroners for this borough, on view of the body of Robert Haxell, who was unfortunately killed the day before by a chimney falling upon him, whilst he was at work in the yard belonging to the Curriers Arms public house in this town. The deceased formerly kept the above house, and was very much respected by all who knew him.

Haxell was 70 years old at the time of his death. The Curriers Arms, which has long since been demolished, stood on Curriers Lane which runs parallel to Civic Drive in the centre of Ipswich.

Undoubtedly one of the oddest and most inconceivable cases of accidental death occurred in Eye in 1806.

On Whitsun Tuesday, the following melancholy accident happened at Eye. As some labourers were amusing themselves by throwing at ten pins, a poor girl about seven years of age attempted to run across the ground, and not being perceived in time by a person who was at that instant in the act of delivering the bowl, it struck the child so violently, directly between the eyes, that she languished in the greatest agonies till Saturday, when she expired.

On the same day, a young man suffered a fate that would become all too common amongst the travelling workforce of the county.

> On Tuesday as Robert Davy, a young man in the service of Mr Wm. Turner, of Old Newton, was returning from Stowmarket, with a wagon heavy loaded; in ascending a hill at Stowupland, he was forced down by the shafts, and both wheels going over his body, he was so dreadfully bruised, that he expired on the following day.

An incident involving a cart or a waggon was always likely to prove fatal because of its huge weight. Robert Davy was 18 years old and was buried in Mendlesham churchyard.

Before the introduction of the Burial Act of 1823, suicides were still treated as a criminal act, as can be evidenced by this report in the Ipswich Journal in 1809 from Colchester in Essex. Although the case occurred outside Suffolk, it serves as an early example of how a suicide was dealt with by the authorities at that time.

> On Thursday the 30th Nov. an inquisition was taken at Colchester, by Frank Abell, Gent., on view of the body of James Reynolds, a corporal in the 1st battalion of the 28th regt. of foot, who on the morning of the preceding day, blew his brains out with a musket. In consequence of the deliberate manner in which the deceased put an end to his existence, by tying one end of a string to the trigger of the piece, and the other end to his foot, by

which means the gun was made to explode under his chin, the Jury found a verdict of felo-de-se, and the body was buried in the King's highway.

The literal translation of the phrase felo-de-se is a 'felon of himself'. In early English common law, an adult who committed suicide was a felon and the crime was punishable by forfeiture of property to the King and what was considered a shameful burial – typically with a stake through the heart and with a burial at a crossroads (in the King's highway). Burials for 'felo de se' usually took place at night, with no mourners or clergy present and the location was often kept secret by the authorities.

Accidents with guns were no less frequent than deliberate acts of violence as can be divined from this 1809 report here following.

> One of those fatal accidents which so frequently occur from having guns and pistols loaded happened very lately at Wickham Market. A young man who had walked over from Framlingham to meet his aged parents, who resided at Wickham, happened to take up an old gun which was occasionally used in keeping off birds, etc. The piece went off in his hands and, shocking to relate, the contents were lodged very near the heart of the old woman, who languished from 5 o'clock in the afternoon till the next morning and then expired.

The reader will have noticed that no names were given in the report. The poor man who accidentally shot his mother must have been devastated, as the immediate family must have been.

Just occasionally, a tragic event occurs which effects a characteristic charitable response from the wealthier inhabitants of the county, that it affects a glow in our hearts. Such an occasion transpired in February 1810 when the country was fighting for its survival against the mighty armies of Napoleon Bonaparte.

> On Saturday the 3rd inst., a most melancholy accident happened at Mendham, near Harleston in Norfolk. As an industrious man, a wheelwright, of the name of Cornish, of Wilby, in this county, with his 15 year old son, were proceeding home with a load of timber, for want of due precaution in loading it, in going down Borking-hill, the carriage was suddenly precipitated on the horses, and in their exertions to stop it, it went over both the father and the son; the former had his right thigh and left leg badly fractured, the latter several ribs broken, and both of them were otherwise so dreadfully bruised and wounded that they survived but a short time. A subscription is set on foot for the widow and family.

The subscription notice in the next edition read as follows:

> The Benevolent and Humane are earnestly entreated to afford their Aid in raising a SUBSCRIPTION for the Relief of the WIDOW CORNISH and Family of Wilby, who by the melancholy accident of losing her Husband and a Son, is bereft of almost every means of support, and in addition to the poignant distress of a situation so afflicting, she is in daily expectation of being confined with her Twenty-second child.

Little wonder that there was a worry that this family would be 'bereft of every means of support', with up to twenty-one children to take care of. Thankfully, by May 1810, over £250 was in the hands of the appointed Trustees. As an example of the liberality of the local middle classes, Mr. Samuel Ray Esq. of Worlingworth gave two guineas.

The former Wilby Swan

The author has no evidence to inform the reader of what happened to the family in the aftermath of this tragedy but the burial records tell us that John, the father, 50 years old and Samuel, the son, 15 years old, were interred in Wilby churchyard and that the widow Charlotte expired just ten years later.

Interestingly, in March, one month after the Mendham tragedy, the following calamitous event in a neighbouring parish to Wilby was reported in the Ipswich Journal. We shall see many further examples of this type of shocking occurrence in the family home during the 19th century. It would be many years before the authorities took action to reduce the occurrence of such avoidable deaths.

> Monday last a child of Samuel Wright's, blacksmith of Horham, near Stradbrook, about 2 years of age, being left in the house with another child while the mother was gone for some milk, although but for a few minutes, its clothes caught fire, and was so much burnt that it survived but a few hours.

Newspapers were not always accurate in their reporting of sudden deaths. For the record, the child's name was Phoebe Wright; she died on Monday March 26th and her parents names, as given in the Horham parish burial register, were Henry and Mary Wright (late Groom).

It was becoming apparent that the hearth or fireplace was a very hazardous place in the cottager's home. The reporting of such deaths in the newspapers led to a greater awareness about the issue for the readership (the middle classes) but no concerted action to educate the masses (the working classes).

Sudden death and the misery that ensued affected all classes of society and this small notice in the 'Deaths' column of the Ipswich Journal in June 1811 did not escape attention.

> A few days since died suddenly, immediately after the operation of bleeding in the arm, the Hon. Countess of Aldborough.

An article in the Gentleman's Magazine about her brother-in-law, Edward Stratford, Earl of Aldborough in Ireland, described her departing scene, as follows:

'She was the toast of the Irish Metropolis, and was the best horsewoman in Ireland. About three months since, her health declining, she visited Bath, where she died. On application to the Faculty, bleeding was advised, an operation to which her Ladyship was unwilling to submit. However she consented and her eyes were covered, her arm bound, and her footman employed to hold her. The instance she felt the lance, her screams so terrified the servant that he let go his hold, and falling on the point of her elbow, whilst the blood was flowing, gave a sudden turn to the current which produced an abscess that baffled medical skill and deprived fashionable society of one of its most fascinating ornaments.'

One should not perhaps forget the deaths that were not as sudden as some, but nevertheless displayed in the death notice that literary touch, which hinted at the qualities of the deceased and remain as testament to that person. In March 1818, a death notice described the earthly qualities of Lydia Ling of Otley Hall.

Thursday last died, in her 71st year, after three months painful suffering, Lydia, the wife of Mr. S. Ling of Otley Hall; her life afforded a constant scene of practical charity and unostentatious benevolence; her death will deprive the world of an excellent example – her husband

and children of an excellent wife and mother – and the poor of a liberal benefactress.

Otley Hall

Returning to our theme, we find, in late December of 1818, what may have been described in recent years as a cot death.

On Friday last, an inquisition was taken at Brundish before Wm. Garnham, Gent., Coroner, for the Liberty of the Duke of Norfolk, on view of the body of George Watling, an infant of the age of 13 weeks, son of James Watling of that place, shoemaker, who was found dead in bed on the preceding Monday. It appeared that the child was left quite well in bed in the morning when the father and mother got up; the latter went out and was gone about an hour, and on her return she and her husband got their breakfasts, after which she went up stairs to fetch the child, when it was found to be dead.

The mother when she got up laid the child upon its side, but when she found it dead, it was lying upon its face. From several circumstances, suspicion had attached upon the father, but after a long investigation, and the evidence of a surgeon, no proof could be adduced to incriminate him. Verdict – "Found dead."

The timeline of this sad event was distressing; the child died on the 21st December and was buried on the 27th. So the inquest took place on Christmas Day.

In 1819, there were two sudden deaths which occasioned inquests in the parish of Worlingworth. The first inquest, in March, concerned a young man who was quite literally struck down in the prime of his life.

On Saturday last, an inquest was held at Worlingworth, before Wm. Hammond, Gent., Coroner, on the body of John Mayhew, who on the Thursday before was killed by a flash of lightning in a severe thunderstorm, whilst working with his father in a field belonging to Mr. Mutimer in that parish. Verdict to that effect.

Mayhew was only 16 years old. A few months later, another youth was killed in the parish. Jeremiah Hill was just 17 years old.

On Monday last, an inquest was held at Worlingworth, before Wm. Hammond, Gent., Coroner, on the body of Jeremiah Hill, who on the Saturday preceding, was riding on the shafts of his master's wagon going to a field to cart home some wheat. The horses being unruly ran away, and the deceased, in attempting to get down to stop them, fell off the shafts near to the fore wheel, which passing over his body occasioned his death a few minutes after. Verdict – Accidental death.

It was prohibited by law to stand or ride on the shafts of a wagon. This was one of the very few laws in place, relating to travel on the King's Highway (along with lewdness and vagrancy).

4

Inquest Reporting from 1820 to 1830

By the 1820s, the newspaper reporting of coroners inquests in some of the lesser-known Suffolk parishes was becoming a feature of the 'Local Intelligence' column of the newspaper. During the month of March 1821, three local inquests in one article were reported in the Ipswich Journal.

> At Stowmarket, on the 8th inst. on the body of Ann Willett, who expired in the bake-office of Mr. Edward Lockwood, in that parish, on the Tuesday preceding, as she was going to pat some dough into the oven to be baked. Verdict – "Natural Death." (She was 63 years old.)

> On the 11th, at Worlingworth, on the body of John Goddard, a poor boy, aged 10 years. It appeared that the deceased and Samuel Mayhew (servant to Mr. Farrow, miller) were going in a cart on the Friday preceding to several parishes for grist. They stopped at the Lion Inn in Bedingfield where Mayhew put into the cart a bottle containing half a gallon of gin for his master. They then proceeded to Southolt, at which place Mayhew left the deceased in the cart, and during his absence, the latter drank a considerable quantity of the gin, which occasioned his death a few hours after. Verdict to that effect.

The same day, at Stoke Ash, on the body of Isaac Elmer, aged 18, who was found drowned in that parish. He was the son of a labourer at Gislingham and was subject to violent fits, by which his intellects were much impaired. Verdict – "Found drowned."

Amongst the various ways of taking one's own life in those depressed agricultural times, poisoning oneself would seem to have been difficult and expensive to plan for and painful to fully execute. Arsenic left the sufferer in great pain for hours before eventual death but in at least one instance, suicide by arsenic poisoning was carried out and the case was reported in the press. One such case resulted in another inquest at the Falcon Inn, Earl Soham.

Inquisition on Thursday last, at Earl Soham, by Mr. Wood jun., on the body of William Pettit (28), of that parish, dish turner. It was proved in evidence that Pettit had purchased at Framlingham, only the day before, half an ounce of white arsenic, under a false pretence, and on being dreadfully ill the same night, acknowledged he had eaten the arsenic he had bought, from the effects of which he died in a few hours. The Jury being satisfied with the evidence proving his insanity, returned a verdict accordingly.

One cannot spare the reader from having distressing thoughts when he or she reads of some of the shocking events that resulted in parish inquests in the early 19th century. In November 1823, we learn of the case of the death of two infants, left momentarily to their own devices, near the open fireplace within each family dwelling.

On Friday, the 7th inst. at Friston, on the body of Lewis Utting (also spelt Utton), a child three years old, son of John Utting, of that parish, labourer. It appeared that in the afternoon of Wednesday the 5th inst., the mother of the deceased had placed a kettle of water upon the fire in her cottage, which she was obliged to leave for a few minutes, and during her absence, the child drank from the spout of the kettle a quantity of the boiling water, which caused his death in the course of a few hours.

On Tuesday last, at Kenton, on the body of Charles Smith, a child about four years old (son of Robert Smith, of that parish, labourer) who set fire to his clothes about 3 o'clock in the afternoon of Saturday the 8th inst. in attempting to reach across the grate. His father was in bed in the same room, but too ill to render him any assistance.

The shrieks of the child brought in a poor neighbour, but he being unfortunately nearly blind, was equally unable to extinguish the flames; his wife, however, came almost immediately to his assistance, and wrapped the child in her mantle, but he was so dreadfully burnt that he died about 9 o'clock the following morning. Jurors verdict in both cases – "Accidental death."

The old Kenton Crown

In the case of Robert Smith's child, it would seem that the fates were entirely working against this poor boy. His father was bed-ridden and the neighbour who attempted to help was almost blind. It is broadly accepted by social historians that the open fireplace in the worker's cottage was one of the most dangerous places within the rural environment. We shall learn of further cases of infant and child deaths involving the setting alight of clothing near to the fireplace throughout the first half of the 19th century. Sadly it was not just the children who suffered such a horrid end to their existence as we learn from a newspaper report in March of that same year, 1823.

> At Occold, on the body of Susan Everson, aged 73 years, who, about 8 o'clock on Sunday morning last, was found lying dead near the grate in the lower room of the house, and burnt in a most shocking manner. Her

37

husband, aged 84 years and upwards, who had been confined to his bed for several years, having lost the use of his limbs, deposed that the deceased, about 7 o'clock the preceding evening, went downstairs to make up the fire, promising as soon as the coals got alight she would put them into the warming pan, and come to bed directly; he having told her not to sit up late. About 8 o'clock he smelt something burning below, in consequence of which he knocked and called, but to no effect; and hearing no noise in the house, he concluded that his wife was burnt to death.

About 8 o'clock the next morning, he was heard by John Runacles, who lives in the adjoining house, calling out for help. Runacles went up to the end of the house, where the poor old man resided, who told him to break open the door, as he was sure his wife was burnt to death. He accordingly broke it open and found the deceased in the state above described, with the warming pan and a candlestick lying close by her side. The deceased being very feeble and infirm, the Jury were of the opinion that she fell down as she was putting more coals in the warming pan, by which means her clothes caught fire and brought her to a melancholy end. Verdict – "Accidental death."

Whilst much of the detail of these cases may be considered astonishing by the standards today, one must sympathise deeply with the plight of the poor labourer and his family in those times of deep poverty and worldly ignorance. We should bear in mind how extremely difficult life must have been for these poor folk and how vulnerable they were to the hidden dangers lurking in the cottage home.

The agricultural workplace was (and remains) an area of industry where the majority of fatal accidents occurred. In the summer of 1823 at Dennington, a most shocking occurrence was reported.

Last Thursday week, James Hart (25), a servant in the employ of John Barker Esq., of Tannington Place, in this county, had both legs dreadfully broken, by the wheels of a tumbrel load of gravel, passing over them in coming out of Mr. Pipe's pit at Dennington; the poor fellow's sufferings in conveying him to his master's house, a distance near 4 miles, were most excruciating; and although every attention was paid him, he died the Saturday following.

Tannington Place, the home of John Barker, Esq.

The year 1824 saw examples of sudden deaths that were extremely common, the reporting of which became more of a feature of the weekly local news. By this time the Ipswich Journal, though still featuring many advertisements and court and parliamentary news, was beginning to report more local news than ever before. The two examples of sudden deaths referred to are reproduced below.

On Monday (in July 1824) an inquest was held at Wilby before Wm. Hammond, Gent., Coroner, on the body of Phoebe Andrews, aged between 3 and 4 years. The deceased, on Saturday last, went with her brother, about 2 years old, to play in the road; she left him soon after and ran to a pond close by, into which she unfortunately fell and was drowned.

On Wednesday last (in December), an inquest was held at Worlingworth before Wm. Hammond, Gent., Coroner, on the body of Samuel Haward aged 55, who was found dead in a field in that parish, on Sunday last. Verdict – "Died by the Visitation of God."

This last verdict was a common one, originally signifying that the cause of death was inexplicable and it was thought that God had decided that it was time for the person to die. It later came to mean that the person had died of natural causes and it was a verdict often given by a coroner's jury. It was very rare for an autopsy to be carried out on a body; instead the doctor would give his opinion on the death, based upon the physical evidence of the body before him and the evidence of the health of the deceased that he heard from others.

From September 1st 1837, the registration of births, marriages and deaths became compulsory by law. In order to bring some statistical order to the reports made by the Registrar General, who compiled these reports on the numbers of such events, Coroners were instructed that the cause of death, in future, was to be made in precise terms and terms such as 'visitation of God' and 'natural causes' were to be avoided if more precise terms could be used. As we shall read later in the book, this did not entirely stop the practice of ascribing a death to the hand of God.

We have already learnt something of the potential dangers involved in driving carts and tumbrils. In 1824, the landlord of the Lion Inn at Little Glemham met with an unexpected and unfortunate end involving his own cart and too much drink.

> Wednesday last an inquisition was held at the Bell Inn, Saxmundham, before Mr. Wood, jun. on the body of Thomas Smith (69), many years hostler at that house. The deceased has for several years past kept the Lion public house at Little Glemham and went to Saxmundham (according to his annual custom) to receive his rents and pass a jovial day among his old acquaintances, and having drank freely, towards the evening became intoxicated and went to sleep in the bar at the Bell for an hour and a half.

> When he awoke he was considerably refreshed but it was past midnight and all offers of a bed were refused; neither would he be persuaded to let any person accompany him home. He left the Bell at half-past one in a common square cart, and drove out of the yard very

well, but had not proceeded more than 100 yards before he fell out, and pitching upon his head, was rendered totally insensible. For 24 hours he remained in that state and then breathed his last. Verdict – "Accidental death."

1825 saw a range of sudden deaths being reported in the press, from general infirmity to determined suicide, of which the latter may have been caused by post-natal depression. These reports included the following; one from July and one from November.

Ufford Street, Melton

On the following day at Melton, on the body of Mary Rout (22), single woman, about 3 months since this girl was delivered of an illegitimate child, and was afterwards in a very dangerous and dying state. She had been returned to her father's roof about 2 months but from being lively and high-spirited became low, melancholy and desponding, and was scarcely ever left by herself. That morning, however, it happened that her father and mother, the maid servant and the boy all left the house after some particular occupation, and she took the advantage of their absence to get into the hay-loft, where she hanged herself with a top latchet. Her body was discovered in about half an hour, just as a surgeon was passing the house, but life was quite extinct. The Jury being perfectly satisfied as to her lunacy returned a verdict accordingly.

On Wednesday last, an inquest was held at Wickham Market by Mr. Wood jun., on the body of Martha Hammond, aged two years eight months, who died on the preceding Monday, from having drank boiling water out of a teakettle standing upon the fireplace during the momentary absence of her mother in an adjoining room. Verdict – Accidental death.

At the beginning of 1826, an accident occurred which prompted the Ipswich Journal to question the wisdom of a practice that had been going on during many previous winters. Although the accident occurred in a different county, the newspaper editor saw fit to report the case in the Ipswich Journal for the benefit of its own readership and to proffer advice, even though it was less than a single line and was therefore unlikely to persuade the masses to make changes to their habits of a lifetime.

Caution against the use of Charcoal in Bedrooms
Last week a very excellent servant of Colonel Gossett at Portsmouth went to bed in perfect health, and was found dead the next morning – he had placed a pan of

charcoal in his room: this imprudence is too often practised, and generally ends fatally.

Of course, we should remember that all of the printed newspapers in Suffolk were not read by the people whose lives were affected most by the sudden deaths that would have devastated their families – the poor.

The vast majority of the poor, even if they had been able to obtain a newspaper, would probably not have been able to read it anyway and so any intended advice about not using charcoal in a confined space or the prudence of using a fireguard in the fireplace would have been unlikely to reach those needing the advice most.

Two further sudden deaths were reported beneath the charcoal warning, the circumstances of which were unusual.

On Thursday 12th inst., (January 1826) at Woodbridge, on the body of Sarah Hayward, single-woman, whose death was mentioned in last week's paper. This young woman, nearly 20 years of age, went to bed with her sister about half-past 11 o'clock the preceding evening in perfect health, and when the sister arose the following morning, the deceased was in bed apparently sleeping, but after being called several times by the family, was discovered quite dead. A medical gentleman, who was examined upon the inquest, expressed his decided opinion that the deceased had died from the sudden visitation of God. Jurors verdict accordingly.

On Friday last at Debenham, on the body of Edmund Moore, late of Earl Stonham, butcher, aged 79 years. It appeared that the deceased had been at Debenham on the 5th inst.; and about 4 o'clock that afternoon, left the Eight Bells public house quite sober and walked away in the direction of his own house. He was not again heard of until Wednesday the 11th inst. when he was found frozen to death in a ditch in Debenham about a mile and a half from the Eight Bells.

In consequence of the severity of the weather, his body was so firmly fixed in the ice that it was removed with difficulty. The Jury being satisfied that the said Edmund Moore, having missed the footpath, had fallen by accident into the ditch where he had evidently remained for nearly 6 days, returned a verdict accordingly.

William Hammond, the County Coroner must have spent a lot of his time trotting across High Suffolk. On November 9th, he was in Fressingfield and the next day he was conducting an inquest at the Bedfield Dog tavern.

Thursday the 9th inst. an inquest was held at Fressingfield on the body of James Carter (40), who, on the Tuesday preceding, as he was in the act of carrying some coals into a shed there, belonging to Mr. Roe, fell down in a fit and instantly expired. Verdict – Died by the Visitation of God.

Fressingfield Workhouse

The former Bedfield Dog Tavern

On the following day another inquest was held before
the same Coroner, at Bedfield, on the body of Daniel

Brock (54), who was drinking with several others at the Dog Inn there, where he was taken violently sick, and died soon after from the effects of liquor. Verdict to that effect.

Before we continue our journey further through the chronology of sudden deaths and learn of the extraordinary happenings in 1827, perhaps we should remind ourselves of some of the ways and means of death that were heard at inquests throughout the county in the previous twenty six years.

Accidentally shot by son
Alcohol poisoning
Bled to death
Burnt to death – clothing set alight
Crushed by a wagon
Drank boiling water
Drowned in a pond
Fell down and expired instantly
Felled by a chimney stack
Fell on one's head
Found dead in a field
Found dead in bed
Fell in a ditch and froze
Hit by a ten pin ball
Run over by a heavy waggon
Struck by lightning
Suffocation from charcoal
Suicide by arsenic poisoning
Suicide by hanging
Suicide by musket shot

A more comprehensive listing of the means of death, recorded through the preservation of Suffolk inquest documents, can be found in the index files at the Suffolk Record Office. The means given above are merely a selection taken from the newspapers of the time.

5

Two Years of Curious Deaths 1827-1828

There was one certainty about sudden deaths recorded in Suffolk – there were no two deaths that were exactly the same and each year brought some completely new 'modus operandi'. However, the years 1827 and 1828 were almost unique for the altogether curious and varied nature of the deaths reported.

In March 1827 came two inquest reports, one of a drowning and the other of an accident at a windmill.

> An inquest was held before Wm. Hammond, Gent., Coroner, on the 22nd inst. at Peasenhall, on the body of Samuel Holmes, aged 18 months, who was found drowned in a rivulet in a meadow near his father's house, who is a farmer in the same parish. The deceased was seen in the yard about one hour before, from whence it was presumed he strayed into the meadow, and going too near the stream, he fell in and was drowned. Verdict accordingly.

> On Saturday last, an inquest was held before Wm. Hammond, Gent., Coroner, at Earl Soham, on the body of John William Madden (20), whose death was occasioned, on the Thursday preceding, by the cogs of one of the wheels in Mr. Symonds's windmill catching his frock as he was in the act of turning up the shaft to screw it tight, when he was unfortunately drawn up by

the wheel and instantly killed. Verdict – "Accidental Death."

The Mill at Earl Soham

In July, another drowning was reported, along with the death of a baby and an unfortunate case of accidental poisoning.

On Monday last an inquisition was taken at Woodbridge, before Mr. Wood, jun. on the body of Joshua Cook, a young man about seventeen years old, an apprentice to Mr. Cook, whitesmith, of that place. The deceased on the preceding afternoon, (with several other young men) was bathing in the river about half a mile from the town – he was not an expert swimmer, and in attempting to swim across the channel, got entangled in some weeds, and immediately disappeared. A boat was instantly got off by his companions, and soon afterwards another, in search of the body, but it was not found for nearly half an hour, and when brought up, life was extinct. Verdict – "Accidentally drowned."

Monday se'nnight an inquisition was held before Simon R. Jackaman, Gent., one of the Coroners of this Borough, at the Shipwrights Arms in this town, on view of the body of Emma Woods, an infant of the tender age of six weeks, whose death was occasioned by the swallowing a cherry, which was inadvertently given her by a lad 11 years old, her brother, who was nursing her and which having lodged in the throat, suffocated her. Verdict accordingly.

A most distressing catastrophe occurred on Friday last at Stoke by Nayland, in the family of Mr. Simpson, a respectable aged farmer, residing near Leavenheath. A quantity of arsenic having been incautiously placed near some flour, was mixed with it in a pudding; Mr. and Mrs. Simpson, a grandson, the servant maid, and two workmen partook of it. The consequences were dreadful – Mr. Simpson died a few hours after, the servant expired in great agony the following morning, Mrs. Simpson, her grandson and the two workmen are recovering, but in a state of severe suffering. The whole would probably have been sacrificed to the deadly mineral but for the very prompt attendance of several surgeons with stomach pumps, etc. An inquest was held on Monday on the bodies of Mr. Simpson and Maria Godfrey, when it clearly appeared that the arsenic was taken by mistake, having been placed by Mr. Simpson in a jar upon a shelf, where some flour had also been put, and the Jury returned a verdict of Accidental Death.

During August, a nasty accident occurred in a barn in Earl Soham. Presumably, the Falcon Inn was busy hosting an inquest again.

On the 29th July, an inquisition was held at Earl Soham before Mr. Wood, jun. on the body of John Brown, of that parish, labourer. About eight o'clock the preceding Friday morning, the deceased was at work for the Rev. Mr. Henchman in his barn-yard, upon a wagon loading straw, which being very dry, about half the load fell down, when Brown falling with the straw came upon a fork (used by another man for pitching the straw) and one of the prongs having penetrated his groin and passing through one of the intestines caused his death in about thirty-six hours. This poor fellow's sufferings were very severe, but the jury were quite satisfied from the evidence that no blame could be attributed to the man pitching, whom the straw completely covered. Verdict – "Accidental Death."

Coroner William Hammond was active in the month of September, with two inquests on the same day about four or five miles apart.

An inquest was held on Monday last, at Stradbrooke, before Wm. Hammond, Gent., Coroner, on the body of Charles Pulham, who was killed on the Friday preceding, by the near wheel of a wagon loaded with wheat, going over him. It appeared he was standing upon the shafts, and in jumping down, the fore wheel caught his heel and threw him down, which occasioned his untimely fate. Verdict – "Accidental Death." On the same day, and before the same Coroner, at Monk Soham, on the body of Mary Davey, who fell down in a fit, as she was sitting in her chair, and instantly expired.

The old Royal Oak at Monk Soham

1828 almost matched the previous year in incident, particularly in respect to the deaths of young children, two of whom fell foul of the perils of the fireplace.

Before Mr. Sparrow, Coroner, on the 15th January at Wrentham, on view of the body of Harriet Roberts, a child about two years old, whose death was occasioned by her having attempted to drink some boiling water from a mug which she had taken off the fire, in doing which she spilled the contents of the mug over her neck and breast, and was so much scalded that she survived but a few days. And on Wednesday last, at Wissett, on view of the body of Charles Curtis, a child about the same age. The deceased, with an elder brother and sister, were left together in a room by their mother, who was absent about half an hour, and in attempting to stir the fire with a stick, his pinafore caught the flame, his clothes were entirely consumed, and the deceased sustained such injury that he died in a few hours. Verdicts in both cases – Accidental Death.

In February, two men found ways to meet their Maker, one quite deliberately at Otley and the other through the demon drink at Lowestoft. During the same period of time, a family tragedy occurred on the banks of the River Gipping.

On Saturday afternoon an inquisition was taken at Otley by Mr. Wood, jun. on the body of Mr. John Cutting, farmer. This unfortunate man, who had been long deranged, attempted to destroy himself, some months since, by driving a large nail into his forehead, but a perfect cure of that wound had been effected; on Saturday morning Mr. Philip Cutting (his brother), who acted as his keeper, left him spreading manure in a field, adjoining the house, and went to a neighbouring farmer's house, from whence he returned in less than half an hour, and found his brother hanging by his silk handkerchief, upon a maple tree, quite dead. Verdict – Lunacy.

On Monday last an inquest was held at Lowestoft before Mr. Sparrow, Coroner, on view of the body of Bartholomew Mewse (18). The deceased met his death from drinking to excess under the following circumstances. A cask of whiskey happened to have been washed ashore at Lowestoft, on Thursday the 14th inst. and the deceased with several other persons on its being landed on the beach, drank profusely of its contents – he was taken home in a state of insensibility from which he never revived. Medical assistance was resorted to, but too late to be effectual. Verdict – died from intoxication. The lives of several other persons were nearly sacrificed by their imprudent indulgence on this occasion, but they have fortunately recovered.

Saturday last as a servant lad of Mr. Jay, at Badley, was returning from Ipswich Market, owing to the darkness of the night, when near his master's house, the cart was turned over and he was seriously hurt. On Monday night, the lad's mother, of the name of Sarah Blyth, had been down Mr. Jay's, and left with her son near dusk to go home, when they had proceeded about 50 rods, in passing a bridge near the lock they both fell into the river, the lad crept out, but the poor woman found a watery grave, leaving a husband and 8 children to regret her unfortunate end; and on Tuesday a man, in the employ of Mr. Jay, had his hand seriously injured by the cogs of a wheel.

Tuesday last an inquest held at Badley Mill, before Mr. Sparrow, Coroner, on view of the body of Sarah, wife of

Daniel Blyth, of Creeting. The deceased came to Badley Mill on the Monday to see her son, who had been much hurt by an accident, and was returning home with him in the evening in great glee from her son's recovery. Their path laid over a bridge on the navigable river near the Mill, but from the darkness of the night, they missed the bridge and both fell into the river below the lock.

The poor woman clung to her son, who with difficulty extricated himself from her grasp and succeeded in swimming to the bank side. He immediately ran to the Mill for assistance, which was speedily obtained, but from the darkness of the night the deceased was not found for nearly an hour after. The usual efforts to restore animation were resorted to by a medical assistant, but without effect. Verdict – Accidental Death.

The victims of this accident on the banks of the river had all of the elements against them. It would have been exceptionally dark and possibly icy. The river might have been in full flood and the water temperature would have threatened life in terms of extended exposure to the cold. Finally we read that the son had to extricate himself from his mother's grasp to save his own life; perhaps a decision that he thought long and hard about in the following months.

During March, we learn of a choking episode, also the sudden death of the girlfriend of Bartholemew Mewse, who took her own life and the almost inevitable report of a child victim of the boiling kettle.

On the 16th inst. an inquest was held at Dennington, in the liberty of his Grace the Duke of Norfolk, before Wm. Hammond, Gent., Coroner, on the body of Henry Heffer, whose death was occasioned by the pressure of a large piece of beef he was in the act of swallowing, resting upon the upper part of the tube conveying the air to the lungs, part of which being forced under the valve covering the tube, produced instant suffocation. Verdict to that effect.

On Monday last, at Lowestoft, before Mr. Sparrow, Coroner, on view of the body of Mary Ann Smith, a young woman, who in a fit of despondency hanged herself. The deceased had been strongly attached to a young man whose death from drinking out of a cask of whiskey that had been washed ashore about a month since, was mentioned in a former paper, and grief at his loss was supposed to have induced the rash act, as from that period she had been inconsolable. Verdict – Insanity.

On Tuesday, at Uggeshall, on view of the body of Robert Roberts, an old man, who suddenly expired in his chair in a fit of apoplexy, while at breakfast. Verdict – Died by the Visitation of God. And on the same day, at Middleton, on view of the body of Howard Chapman, a child of two years old, who, in the momentary absence of his mother, drank out of the spout of a tea kettle of boiling water that was standing on the grate, and was so much injured in the throat, that the child died in a few hours afterwards. Verdict to the above effect.

The former Uggeshall Buck

During the spring of 1828, we read of two child deaths characterised once more by the risks associated with parents taking leave of their children for a short period of time, resulting in the child's injury and death.

In April 1828, on the 7th inst., an inquest was held before William Hammond, Gent., Coroner, at Worlingworth, on the body of Noah Archer, who was so terribly burnt by his clothes catching fire as he was warming himself at the grate, that he survived but a few hours, his mother having left him in the room with two other children whilst she went out to see a sick person. Verdict – Accidental Death.

A crowd outside the General Wolfe Inn, Laxfield

On Monday last (May 19th), an inquest was held at Laxfield before Wm. Hammond, Gent., Coroner, on the body of William Cook, aged 4 years, who was found drowned in a pond adjoining the premises where he resided. It appeared that he was seen in the yard about a quarter of an hour before, with an angling rod and line in his hand, which laid on the steps of the pond, and it was supposed that in attempting to put the string in the water, he unfortunately fell in where he met his untimely fate. Verdict – Found Drowned.

June 1828 saw one of those cases which would set tongues wagging in the neighbourhood of Saxmundham. We have the Ipswich Journal and its diligent reporter to thank for the detail which ultimately still left questions unanswered about the Benhall schoolmaster and his family.

On Friday the 6th June, at Benhall, on the body of a new born male child, which was found the preceding morning concealed up the chimney in the school-room, part of the dwelling house of Robert Brightwell. John Brightwell, aged 13 years and upwards deposed that in his father's absence he and several other boys were at play in the school-room, when he climbed up the chimney for a hoop, which he knew had been hidden there about 3 months before; in searching for the hoop, he found a white bundle, which, after some hesitation and debate among the boys, he pulled down on to the hearth when the legs of a child appeared.

The boys being frightened all ran out and gave an alarm, soon after which the child was carried by Catherine Brightwell, his sister, about 12 years old, out of the school-room into the back kitchen, where it was laid upon the bricks and the white cloth undone in the presence of Mary Brightwell, his mother. It was then plainly discovered to be the body of a male child. That his mother then wrapped it up again in the same cloth, took it down cellar and left it there, and in 10 or 15 minutes afterwards he saw Catherine his sister, and another little girl of the same age, bring up out of the cellar, an earthen pot containing the same white cloth and carry it towards the chamber stairs. The witness deposed to the illness of his eldest sister, Mary Brightwell, about ten days before, and to several other circumstances; and when the parish officers, who had heard strange reports, came to the house, they discovered this child in a dark attic, although the fact of there having been a child found at all was at first denied to them.

Mary Brightwell, wife of Robert Brightwell, Jane Brightwell, the daughter, aged 16 years and upwards, and Catherine Eastaugh, of Friston, widow (who came to the house in consequence of the illness of Mary Brightwell, her granddaughter) were all examined very strictly, but denied any knowledge whatever of the pregnancy of Mary Brightwell, of her delivery, and of the concealment of the child in the chimney, although her pregnancy had for several weeks preceding, been notorious in the parish and the neighbourhood.

Benhall Street - a tranquil scene

Three medical men (one of whom had several times attended Mary Brightwell the daughter, subsequently to the supposed birth of this child, but who gave no evidence of that fact; nor of any circumstances that excited his suspicion as to what had taken place) were also examined, and deposed that from the state of putrefaction in which the body was found it was impossible to give an opinion whether the child had been born alive or not. There was no servant of any kind kept in Brightwell's family and in the absence of all evidence whatever to prove this child to have been born alive, the Jury, consisting of twenty-three most respectable farmers and tradesmen, were unable to return any other verdict than "Found dead." This inquest occupied nearly the whole day and the affair remains enveloped in considerable mystery, exciting much interest in the neighbourhood.

A particularly sad case of suicide followed in July. A case of suicide always seemed to bring out the fine detail of the circumstances by which the deceased achieved their untimely aim, in this case, the hanging of the bonnet on a bough of a tree.

Wednesday last an inquest was held at Mickfield, before Mr. Sparrow, Coroner, on view of the body of Emma Garrard, a servant in the family of Mr. Poole, a respectable farmer in that village. It appeared in evidence that the deceased, on Tuesday morning last, had without any apparent cause or motive whatever, committed suicide, by throwing herself into a moat near the house. She had risen at an early hour with another female servant of the family, and had gone about her work as usual, when about four or five o'clock she was missed, and was immediately sought after, and was found about half past five by a cow boy in a moat close by the house. The deceased had hung up her cap on the bough of a tree that hung over the moat, and had tied herself to the tree by a plough line, one end of which she had fastened around her body, and the other to the trunk of the tree. There being nothing to prove the existence of any exciting cause that led to the rash act, the Jury, after maturely considering the evidence, returned a verdict of felo-de-se and the Coroner issued his warrant for the private interment of the body under the provisions of a late Act of Parliament passed in the 4th year of his present Majesty.

We bring 1828 to a close with the shortest of reports of a sudden death in September, emphasising the dangers associated with brewing.

On the 5th inst. died after 3 weeks of dreadful suffering, occasioned by his fall into a mash-tub of hot liquor, Mr. William Smith, retail brewer, of Horningsheath, aged 51, leaving a widow and nine children to lament their loss.

The county of Suffolk and indeed the wider nation were dangerous places to live in the final years of the reign of George IV. Whether it was in the workplace, in front of the hearth, by the banks of a water course or on the turnpike road, the hazards were many and the poor uneducated agricultural labourer and his family often became the casualties in an unforgiving world. This situation did not improve in the ensuing years. The continuation of the trend of population growth, particularly in urban areas, increased the probability of accidents occurring in all aspects of life.

Before the middle of the 19th century, two other developments complicated the situation—these were the widespread development of the railways and the increasing introduction of machinery to agricultural practices. Before these changes could really take effect, the 1830s came along—a decade of unrest and upheaval.

6

The 1830s - Dissent, Destitution and Disease

As we move into the 1830s, we enter a decade of agricultural unrest characterised by criminal incendiarism. For the poverty-stricken, the outlook remained bleak and, to make matters worse, the poor also endured a series of extremely cold, epidemic-ridden winters.

In September 1830, a new coroner for the liberty of His Grace the Duke of Norfolk was elected. Charles Gross, Gent., was elected to the role by the Freeholders of the County to replace William Hammond, Gent., who had tended his resignation in June 1830. Mr. Hammond had served his area of the county for over thirty years but he had obviously decided that, in his old age, he could not manage the almost interminable mileage that he, his cart and his pony were racking up week in and week out.

October 1830 saw the new Assistant Coroner, Mr. John Wood Jnr., who had succeeded his father, visiting a familiar parish in High Suffolk - Earl Soham.

> Tuesday last an inquisition was taken at Earl Soham, by Mr. Wood, jun. on the body of George Curtis, who was the preceding afternoon, working a chaff engine for his master, Mr. Kent, and in his presence, suddenly dropped down and almost immediately expired. Jurors verdict - Died by the sudden visitation of God. Curtis was only 21 years of age.

In March 1833, a tragedy occurred on the River Waveney near Syleham.

An inquisition was taken before C. Gross, Gent. on Wednesday last, at the parish of Syleham, on view of the body of Eliza Matthews, aged 14 years, who came by her death in the following manner. The deceased was riding on Monday last, with four other children, in a cart, driven by her mother, from Brockdish to Syleham; a stream of water runs across the road about a quarter of a mile from Brockdish, which was at that time unusually deep; when the horse (a blind one) was in the middle of the stream it stopped, and Mrs Matthews touched it with the whip, it sprang forward, broke the belly band, and precipitated the whole six into the water. Mrs Matthews was carried by the stream, which was very rapid, to the other side of the road, and catching hold of the bough of a tree, hung by it till she was taken up in a boat, after having remained in the water more than 20 minutes; the deceased floated down the stream into the river, and was found drowned the next morning.

The four children, with the greatest difficulty, held by the cart till a lad of the name of Wm. Sparrow, who was in a field close by, hearing their cries, came to their assistance and in a most praiseworthy manner, plunged into the stream 5 different times, and landed them in safety. The Coroner said he thought it his duty, as Coroner, to thank him for his exertions, but it is hoped he will receive something more substantial than thanks.

The peaceful Waveney at Syleham

In February 1834, we hear of further 'awful mortality' when two workers dropped dead within an hour of each other.

> We have seldom to record a more melancholy illustration of the important truth, "In the midst of life we are in death," than that which occurred in the establishment of John Cobbold jun. Esq., at the Cliff Brewery, in this town, on Friday se'nnight. The wife of --- Hamilton, an industrious woman, who it was hoped was recovering from her lying-in, while putting on her attire was stricken by the hand of death, and immediately expired. – Saul, the store-house-man, on hearing of the melancholy event, proposed among his fellow-workmen to make a purse to assist Hamilton to bury his wife. Less than half an hour after, while at his work, he also was suddenly taken ill, fell down and died.

It was not just the poor labouring families who experienced the premature hand of death – even the parish priest was affected. In February 1836, a local cleric suffered a dreadful accident in London from which there was no chance of recovery.

> On 5th February, in London, the Rev. Samuel Loney Barker, chaplain to the Duke of Cambridge and of Tannington, in this county. The death of the reverend gentleman was caused under the following melancholy circumstances. He was crossing over at the corner of Regent-street, Oxford-street, when he was thrown down by a runaway horse; he was immediately conveyed to the shop of Mr. Bridges, chemist, in Regent-circus, where every attention which medical skill could devise, was administered by two medical gentlemen who were passing at the time the accident occurred; but medical aid proved unavailing, the unhappy gentleman's scalp having been torn from the frontal bone, which depressed in and fractured the longitudinal sinews. The animal which occasioned this fatal accident was ridden by a boy, and died within an hour after the accident, from an injury it received in running against the wheels of a dray; the boy was severely injured by falling against the dray.

In May of that same year, we learn of further fatalities with which the reader is becoming increasingly familiar. The inquests ranged across the county from Thwaite, Worlingworth and Weybread in the north to Lavenham in the south and Ousden near Bury St. Edmunds.

On the 16th May 1836: before C. Gross, Gent., at Thwaite, on view of the body of Amy Rush, who, on the morning previous, was found dead in bed; there were no marks of violence appearing on her body, and no doubt but that she died of a fit of apoplexy. Verdict – Died by the Visitation of God.

The Buck's Head at Thwaite

And on the 18th inst., at Worlingworth, on view of the body of George Beecroft, who on the day before, hanged himself in a barn in that parish; the deceased had frequently laboured under fits of temporary derangement, and on one occasion attempted to drown himself. Verdict – Lunacy.

On the 17th, at Lavenham on John Ambrose, a child aged 6 years, who was found drowned in an unenclosed piece of water by the side of the road near his father's house and into which it is supposed he must have accidentally fallen.

Ousden Hall

On the 20th, at Ousden, on Edward Lowe, aged 40 years, who was bathing in the moat belonging to the Hall, and being seized with the cramp, was drowned before any assistance could be rendered him. Verdict in each case – Accidental death.

On the 22nd at Weybread, on view of the body of Wm. Hancy, who on the previous day, was killed by the overturning of a wagon laden with bark. It appeared that the deceased had contracted for the carting of the bark which was very badly loaded; when he came to the stream of water which divides the counties of Norfolk and Suffolk, he stopped the horses, intending to walk over the footbridge whilst his son rode the fore horse; the instant the wagon stopped, it overturned and forced him into the water; he was dead before he could be taken out. Verdict accordingly.

And on the 25th at Worlingworth, on view of the body of Mary Fisher, who on the Monday previous, whilst walking upon the public road there, was accidentally forced to the ground by the nave of the near wheel of a tumbrel, laden with corn, and driven by George Atkins, who was riding therein, by means thereof she instantly died. Verdict – Accidental death.

In April 1837, the coroner returned to Worlingworth once again. This particular case illustrated the dangers to children in agricultural work. Indeed, would we, today, allow a teenager to have sole responsibility for a waggon and team of horses?

An inquest was held at Worlingworth, on Monday last, by Charles Gross, Gent. Coroner, on view of the body of John Smith, aged 14, who, whilst driving a team, on the 4th inst., in that parish, accidentally fell from the shafts of the waggon, when melancholy to relate, the near wheel passed over his body. The sufferer lingered in great agony for two days, and then expired. Verdict - Accidental death.

Suicides and tragic accidents were not the only causes of inquests - tomfoolery in the workplace endangered many lives and one young man was disabled for life following a silly prank at work in Peasenhall in July 1838.

> On Saturday last a very serious accident happened at Mr. Smith's Drill Manufactory, Peasenhall, to two young men in his employ. On the previous day. Mr. Smith overheard the men say they would have a good blow on Saturday, by filling an old iron weight, which was hollow, with gunpowder. Mr. S. took the weight away, and laid it, as he thought, where the men would not find it. But on the Saturday morning one of the men found it, took it unknown to Mr. S., and secreted it until noon. Whilst the men were gone to dinner, the two men before alluded to put 2 ounces of gunpowder into the hollow of the weight and a wood plug over it; then taking a large nail to drive in by the side of the plug, they made use of a hammer, which instantly struck fire, and the powder exploded with a tremendous noise.

> The consequence was, Row, the young man who was driving the nail, had a part of three fingers and his thumb blown off his left hand, his wrist broken, and his face burnt in a shocking manner, and it is very doubtful whether he will ever have his sight again. The other man had his face burnt very much and was otherwise seriously injured. Row had been married only three weeks.

Further inquests in 1838 again bring into focus the potential for deaths to occur in ponds and rivers, whether by accident or deliberately self-inflicted. It might appear from the detail of these reports that the columnist of the newspaper considered his readership to have a fascination with deaths in and around water.

At Rattlesden, on the 9th instant, on the body of Elizabeth Moore, aged about 37, who was found by her husband, drowned in a pond near his house, at an early hour on that morning.

It appeared, from the evidence of Robert Moore, higgler, the husband, that he went to bed the night before between nine and ten o'clock; that the deceased suckled her infant, and was standing at the window when the witness fell asleep; he awoke about two o'clock in the morning, and, missing his wife, got up and searched the house; he was afterwards employed for some time in assisting two boys with a cart, which they could not get along the stones on the road; and then went to two ponds, at the second of which he found his wife's bonnet on the bank, and her body lying in the water near the edge. He went for assistance and the body was taken out, quite dead, and, he believed, had been dead some time.

The deceased had been low-spirited at times during the last two years, and was very low on Sunday. About two years ago, witness put her out of temper, and she went into the churchyard, and said she must make away with herself. He was reduced in circumstances, and they were much distressed in the winter; and he thought that preyed on her mind. Verdict - Temporary Derangement.

The Brewers Arms, Rattlesden

Evidence of the utter despondency with which ordinary people suffered in their daily lives is exemplified by these next inquests relating to two suicides.

On the 8th inst., at Rickinghall Superior, on Mary Wilby, aged 18 years, who, the day preceding, hanged herself with her apron, on a beam in an out-house of the premises of her master, Mr. George Porter. It appeared in evidence that she had been in Mr. Porter's service about three months; that in her former service, she had misconducted herself, and in consequence was discharged, and that Mr. Porter had kindly taken her with a view of reclaiming her; that she was treated with great kindness and attention, be that she was unsettled and lately in a desponding state of mind; and that for some days she had not finished her meals, and when asked the reason by her fellow-servants made no answer, but always expressed her sense of Mr. Porter's kindness to her. No dispute had taken place with any of the family, and no blame had been attached to them, but on the day in question she had hastily risen from dinner, and was missing for some time. On a search being made, she was found hanging as above. Verdict - Temporary Derangement.

The former Bell Inn, Rickinghall Inferior

On the 10th inst., at Weybread, on William Margeram, aged 33 years. He had a wife and four children; his wages were 9s. a week, and his eldest child earned 1s. 6d. a week. After a long investigation, it appeared from the evidence of his fellow-workman, that he had been in a desponding state from the pressure of the times, and that he had been relieved by a pint of beer a day, to the amount of five shillings, by the kindness of the witness, who lived next door. On the morning of the said instant, he was found suspended by his handkerchief, in the privy of the premises occupied by himself. Verdict - Temporary Derangement.

In the present age of street-lighting, headlights and road safety devices, we forget how dangerous the country road at night was to any traveller unfortunate enough to be walking alone. The following inquest report illustrates this.

On the 18th inst., at Horham, on view of the body of William Riches, a man upwards of 70 years of age, who on the night of 2nd of October last, was returning from Stradbroke Sessions, walking in the middle of the road, and being deaf, did not hear a gig approaching, and consequently was knocked down and driven over, and received an injury in his leg, which, after a lingering illness of seven weeks, caused his death on the 15th inst. Verdict - Accidental Death.

7

The Misery and Misfortune of the Hungry Forties

The dawn of the 1840s saw increased news coverage of county inquests. As the newspaper readership increased, so more extraordinary tales of misery and misfortune were required to be published to titillate the reader. No examples could demonstrate more clearly the utter hopelessness of the poor than the stories of Tom Cockerill and Maria Church in July 1840.

On Thursday, at Stratford St. Mary on view of the body of Thomas Cockerill, aged 38. The deceased, as it appeared in evidence, had reached the Anchor Inn, at Stratford, on Sunday evening last, greatly exhausted, having walked that day from Chelmsford, he was without a coat and almost penniless. That evening he slept in a hay loft, but, on Monday, being worse, he was, by order of the Overseer, removed to the house and put to bed; he was also attended by Mr. Spurgin, who found him suffering from an attack of jaundice and administered the proper medicines. He continued in this state till Wednesday morning, when he got up and went out, and was soon afterwards found dead, lying on the floor of the privy. Verdict - Natural Death.

On the 17th ult., at Kenton, on Maria Church, aged 5 years, daughter of David Church of that parish, labourer, whose clothes caught fire on the 7th ult., whilst her mother was gone for their weekly supply of flour and her children were necessarily left by themselves. Church is a very poor man with a pregnant wife and a large family struggling hard to keep out of the Union House and neglected procuring medical assistance for many hours so that his child, after lingering for several days, died from the severe injury she received. Verdict - Accidental Death.

Accidents in the workplace merited some column inches, as in this distressing incident which occurred at Little Blakenham.

A very melancholy accident, attended with loss of life, occurred in the parish of Little Blakenham, on Friday, about 8 o'clock in the morning. Some labourers in the employ of Mr. Bailey, farmer of that place, were engaged in removing bricks from an archway in an old lime kiln at Blakenham, when the bricks gave way and fell upon two men named Lafflin and Piper. The latter was taken out with his thigh broken, and was immediately conveyed to the East Suffolk Hospital, but his unfortunate partner was killed on the spot. Poor Lafflin was an industrious labourer, and has left a widow and nine children to lament his untimely end.

The year 1842 began with a woman and another child burnt to death and a labourer crushed by his waggon.

On the 5th inst., at Wortham, on Mrs. Mary Adams, aged 68, who was burnt to death accidentally. Mr. Adams, the husband of the deceased, and two daughters, had been spending the evening of New Years Day with Mr. Henry Adams, the son, who is also a farmer in that parish. A man and a boy were in the house with the deceased, and about nine o'clock they were ordered by their mistress to go to bed; they went to bed and did not hear any alarm in the night. About one o'clock on Sunday morning, Mr. Adams returned with his two daughters and one son, and found his wife burnt to death, lying upon the floor of the kitchen. A more frightful spectacle was never witnessed.

Benhall Horse and Groom

Same day, on George Storey, horse driver to Mr. William Gobbitt, of Yoxford. On the 18th ult., he had been to Little Glemham for 67 sacks of pollard, and unfortunately got intoxicated. In going down the hill near Mr. Holland's he fell off the shafts and the near wheels went over his left leg, breaking it in two places, and tearing away the flesh of the calf. He was carried to the Benhall Horse and Groom and immediately attended by Messrs. Freeman, who amputated the limb early the following morning, but he died about 15 minutes after the operation. In giving evidence on the inquest, Mr. Robert Freeman said he had never seen such a bad fracture. Verdict - Accidental death, with a deodand on the wheels. Mr. Gobbitt, on hearing of the accident, came over to Benhall, and very humanely remained with the poor man until his death.

A similar incident occurred at Farnham in February.

On the 17th instant, at Farnham, upon James Manby, of Wilby, aged 24 years, servant to Mr. Barnabas Scace, of that place. Manby and another man had, on Tuesday last, been to Iken Cliff with two loads of barley, and were returning with coals, when about a mile from the Farnham George, Manby, being intoxicated, fell down in the road and the two near wheels passed directly across his chest; his partner and one of Mr. Moseley's servants carried him to the public house, where he was attended by two medical men who were of the opinion that Manby could not survive, and he died about two o'clock the following morning. Jurors' verdict: Accidental Death, with a deodand upon the wheels.

Farnham George & Dragon Inn

The fireplace was not the only hazardous feature of the cottager's home, although in the following case, the tragedy probably unfolded in the backhouse of a farmhouse.

> On the 19th March, at Easton, on Jeremiah Franks, aged 3 years, son of Robert Franks, of that parish, labourer. On the preceding morning, Mrs. Franks had been brewing, and the boiling beer just set to cool - having to go into the backhouse where the beer was, the child followed, unperceived by her, she turned around, and in an instant the child fell backwards into one of the keelers, and was scalded to such a degree, that he died the following morning. Verdict - Accidental Death.

Mrs. Sarah Franks was farm servant to John Catchpole, a farmer, and one of her many duties would have been to help with the brewing of beer on the farm. Home brewing was an integral part of Suffolk rural life. The beer produced was only mildly intoxicating and was a wholesome drink for the labourer. The local water supply would often become tainted and beer was preferred to water as the drink of choice. Beer was also brewed in large quantities in time for the harvest home celebrations. Mrs. Franks had to balance the necessity of ensuring that the brewing was successful for her employer, with the needs of her three year son, who probably followed her everywhere she went.

The Easton White Horse

The propensity for sudden deaths to shock the reader would not diminish, as evidenced by the case of a child who was inadvertently poisoned, whilst being treated for worms in 1842.

On the 16th inst., at Debenham, on Susanna Bendall, aged 3 years, daughter of Dennis Bendall, of that place, wheelwright, who died on the preceding day. It appeared in evidence that, in consequence of this little girl being troubled with worms, her mother sent on Thursday afternoon to John Cunnell, who sells drugs, for two worm powders. Mrs. Bendall gave her daughter one early the following morning, who was shortly after seized with excessive drowsiness, and from other strange symptoms. Mr. Locke, the surgeon, was sent for and he immediately pronounced that she had taken some narcotic poison; he administered an emetic and used the stomach pump, but she died about one o'clock, six hours after taking the powder. Enquiries were immediately set on foot, and it was discovered that Cunnell, instead of sending seven grains of rhubarb mixed with two of calomel, as he intended, had sent nine grains of pure opium. Verdict - Accidental Death from taking of opium by mistake.

The enquiry occupied several hours, and the Coroner, at the request of the jury, and a magistrate who was present, gave Cunnell a severe reprimand for his gross negligence and inattention, and advised him to discontinue selling such dangerous drugs. It is much to be lamented that persons should be suffered to sell medicine without previously passing some examination as to their qualifications.

Two more inquests that month dealt with another child being burnt to death and a young man being accidentally shot.

On the 18th at Rushmere on William Mann, aged four years, who had been left by his grandmother (with whom he lived), in the afternoon of the 15th, for a few minutes, when his clothes caught fire and were entirely burnt off his body. He lingered until the following evening when he died. Verdict - Accidentally burned. The Coroner told the jury that "he never, in the course of 25 years he has been coroner, saw any person so extensively burnt."

On the 26th inst., at Trimley St. Martin, on Robert Ashwell, aged 17 years. On Thursday 21st, Ashwell, Mallett and Warner were at plough for Mr. Last, when John Gorham came into the field with a crow gun. Warner borrowed the gun but it missed fire; Gorham then took it to put on another cap, and the moment he had done so, the gun went off and lodged the contents in the calf of Ashwell's right leg. The two other men were also within a yard of the gun when discharged. Ashwell was carried home and attended by Mr. Wilkin, the surgeon; but mortification came on and he died on Sunday night. The jury, being quite satisfied that it was purely an accident, returned a verdict to that effect.

The month of July 1842 must have been warm and conducive to swimming in the local watercourses. It heralded more examples of drownings around the county.

On Tuesday last, at Coddenham, on view of the body of John Salter, aged 23, who was found drowned in the River Gipping, near Baylham Mill, on Sunday evening last. The deceased was supposed to have been bathing as his clothes were found on the bank, but from the depth of the river where he had sunk, he was not found for several hours. Verdict - Found Drowned.

On the following day, at Mendham and Weybread, near Harleston, on view of the bodies of Mr. George Gedney, of the former place, aged 45 years, and master John Bacon, son of Mr. Bacon, miller, of Weybread, aged 14 years.

It appeared in evidence that the latter had been spending the day at Mendham, with Mr. Gedney's sons, when in the evening, after ten, the youths proposed bathing in the river nearby; this was objected to by Mr. Gedney, but who afterwards consented to their going, and resolved to accompany them from fear of danger. The lads took the river where it was shallow, the deceased, John Bacon, preceding them, when he suddenly fell into a hole and sunk. This was perceived by Mr. Gedney, who sprang from his pony and rushed into the river to rescue the poor lad, who, grasping hold of Mr. Gedney, drew him down with him, and both were drowned.

Immediate assistance was at hand; the bodies were brought on the bank, and every means used that medical skill could suggest to restore animation, but which were unavailing. The deceased youth was a remarkably fine lad and Mr. Gedney has left a wife and six children to deplore his loss.

To bring 1842 to a close, a particularly sad suicide was reported from Sweffling.

> On the 6th inst., at Sweffling, on the body of Jonathan Hall, aged 70 years, who hanged himself in a bullock shed, in that parish the preceding morning. Hall had buried his wife only a few days before and had fixed to sell off his little furniture and go into the Plomesgate Union workhouse. These circumstances, added to his previous low melancholy state of mind, induced him to commit suicide. Verdict - Lunacy.

The beginning of 1843 brought the attention of the newspaper readership to two shooting accidents in January.

> An accident of a lamentable nature, which occurred on Tuesday last, in this town (Ipswich), has plunged a most respectable family into much affliction. In the early part of the afternoon of that day, Frederick, son of Mr. Robert Fisk, merchant, Common Quay, about 16 years of age, was engaged in shooting rats at the back of his father's premises. By means of a ladder he got upon a wall about ten feet in height, when, shocking to relate, as he was about sitting down, the gun he had in his hand accidentally went off, and he received the contents of the charge in his leg, just below the knee.

> Immediate assistance being at hand, the unfortunate youth was removed into his father's house, and Mr. Bartlett and Mr. Hammond, surgeons, being sent for, the wound was examined, when it was found that the

arteries were so much lacerated and the bone so dreadfully shattered, that instant amputation was necessary in order to save the life of the sufferer. The operation was very successfully performed, and we are happy to say that the patient, who is a very promising youth and an only son, is likely to recover.

On Wednesday last, as Mr. John Claxton (34), of Stradbroke, was concealed in a shed for the purpose of shooting sparrows, his gun accidentally went off, and shot him completely through the body, and he expired about half an hour afterwards. He was relieving-officer to the Hoxne Union, and highly respected by all who knew him. He has left three father-less and mother-less children to lament their loss.

Stradbroke - Queen Street

As provincial newspapers like the Ipswich Journal and the Bury & Norwich Post filled their columns with inquest reports every week, they began to comment on the need for some form of action to protect the young from the preventable deaths that were occurring in the cottagers homes. February 1843 brought yet another case of burning.

> On Tuesday last at Oulton, on view of the body of Mary Ann Baxter, aged 4 years. This is another instance added to the many constantly occurring of the lives of children being sacrificed to the careless habit of leaving them in a room where there is a fire, without due care being taken to prevent accident. In this case it does not appear that the child had been left more than five minutes, but on her mother's return she found the deceased wrapt in flames, and so dreadfully burnt that she survived about two hours only. Verdict - Accidental Death.

In the following month of March 1843, a young married woman lost her life through her clothes catching fire. The servant probably knew no better than to obey her mistress's order to call her husband rather than try to save her mistress's life.

> Before J.E. Sparrow, Gent., Coroner. On Monday last, at Yoxford, on view of the body of Rebecca, the wife of Robert Haward, miller, of that place, aged 24, whose death was occasioned in a most calamitous way, by her clothes accidentally taking fire as she was in the act of taking an iron heater from the stove in the room in which she had been ironing. Her cries brought her servant into the room, whom she desired to call her

husband, who, being nearby, ran into the room, and found her enveloped in flames. He succeeded in extinguishing the flames, but the deceased was so severely burnt, that she survived only till the following day. Verdict - "Accidental Death."

It was not always the most sensational cases of sudden death that were reported. Even the more mundane cases filled the weekly column inches, as in this case from May 1843.

On Friday last, at Clopton, on the body of Francis Woods, labourer, aged 63 years. Woods had been afflicted with a scrofulous complaint in his left leg for a great many years, which was the cause of his being discharged from the Marines. On Thursday afternoon, when alone upstairs, he accidentally received a blow by striking against a bedstead the diseased leg, which bled copiously, and continued to do so until he fainted and fell down on the floor. His situation was then discovered and a doctor sent for, but before medical assistance could be obtained, Woods was dead.

Before the enquiry was entered upon, it was considered that some blame was attached to the parish doctor, but it appeared that he was some miles distant from home and another medical man obliged to go elsewhere. Verdict- "Accidental Death, from excessive bleeding."

The summer of 1843 saw a carting accident occur at Marlesford.

On Thursday last Mr. William Beecroft, of Ufford Crown, Mr. Henry Fisher, of Melton, and Mr. Tice, of the White Hart, Wickham Market, started, a little before 12 o'clock, from the latter place in a phaeton, to attend an auction at Leiston. The horse 7 years old and a steady one, the joint property of Beecroft and Fisher, was driven by the latter, and in descending the hill into Marlesford the carriage came against his hocks and caused him to run away; the driver succeeded in stopping him before they came to Marlesford Bridge. Fisher got out, and after adjusting the harness resumed the reins and started again; they had no sooner passed the crown of the bridge than the horse started off at full speed.

Mr. Tice, who sat by the driver, caught hold of the near rein, which instantly snapped; he then jumped out by setting his foot on to the step, fell down in the road and escaped unhurt. Fisher threw himself into the hedge on the other side and also fell uninjured; but Mr. Beecroft, who was a stout heavy man, in attempting to get out behind, fell and pitching on his head may be said to have been killed on the spot, as he was picked up senseless, bleeding profusely and expired in a few minutes. An inquest was held the same evening before Mr. Wood and a respectable jury, when these melancholy facts were fully proved by the evidence of Mr. Tice, Mr. Fisher, and James Cornish, a shoemaker, at Marlesford, who was an eye-witness. Verdict - "Accidental death." Deodand 2s.

Further up the turnpike road in August 1843, at Wickham Market, a minor tragedy began and developed into something of a 'local controversy'. Fortunately, the gentleman's surname was not alluded to.

> On Tuesday last at Wickham Market, on the body of John Starkes, aged 11 years. It was proved before the jury that Starkes, accompanied by a younger boy, went that morning to bathe in the river Deben, and getting out of his depth, was unfortunately drowned. A gentleman entered the field soon afterwards, and saw the poor boy lying at the bottom of the river, in less than 5 feet water, without attempting to get out the body, and 10 minutes more elapsed before another man came up, who immediately got him out, but life was then quite extinct.

> The jury after returning a verdict of "Accidentally drowned", commented in strong terms upon the conduct of the individual alluded to, for although it is impossible to say whether the life of this poor boy could have been saved, still the attempt ought to have been made.

During the same month, a man in his late fifties inexplicably met his death amongst a herd of cows.

> On Monday last, at Brundish, on the body of Philip Cracknell. The deceased was a farming servant in the employ of Mrs. Button, of that place, and early on the preceding Friday left his bedroom at the usual hour in

the morning, apparently in a good state of health, and proceeded to fetch up the cows, but not returning with them, he was searched for and found dead in the cow yard. Verdict - Natural Death.

In December 1843, at Blaxhall, a teenage boy took his own life after he was accused of stealing.

On Tuesday last, at Blaxhall, on the body of Henry Bailey, aged 13 years, servant boy to Mr. Hillen, at the Lime Tree Farm. On Sunday, a friend who came to the house, went to lunch with the family, leaving his great coat in the kitchen. On taking it at night he missed 5d in copper from the pockets. This boy, who had alone been left in charge of the same, had then gone home to sleep. Very early the following morning, Louisa Gowing, the dairy maid, charged him with not only stealing the half pence, but some apples from her, and threatened to send for the policeman.

Bailey admitted he had stolen the apples, but denied the other charge; and instead of stopping in the house to breakfast, went out at 6 o'clock and hanged himself, by means of a cow shackle to a beam in the neat house loft. He was searched for all day in vain, but found late in the afternoon, and immediately cut down, his body being stiff and cold. After an examination of witnesses to prove these facts, the jury returned a verdict of felo-de-se, and he was, under the Coroner's directions, buried in Blaxhall churchyard the same evening, as provided by the late Act. It was afterwards satisfactorily proved that Bailey had taken the half-pence.

The years 1843 and 1844 were the peak years of rural incendiarism in East Anglia with over 300 fires reported. There were many reasons for this alarming criminality but it is not the purpose of this book to explore those reasons; suffice to say that relations between the labourer and his master, the farmer, were at a very low ebb. Newspaper reporting of these sensational incendiary acts took up many column inches at the expense of other newsworthy items.

The reporting of coroners inquests was largely discarded in 1844 where the subjects of unrest and incendiarism in the countryside were such hot topics. We must now move on to the year 1845 to resume our perusal of those sudden and sensational deaths which occurred in our county and which merited space in the newspapers.

8

1845 onwards: Railways - a New Hazard

As we neared the middle of the century, it would be appropriate to mention how society was modernising and developing. The population of rural parishes was about to peak in 1851. Commerce was increasing. Migration and emigration was increasing. Railways in Suffolk were expanding rapidly, as were port facilities such as those at Ipswich. Medical science was advancing in leaps and bounds though there was evidence for the misuse of narcotic drugs, such as laudanum being used on children within the household.

Incendiarism was on the decline but criminality was still on the increase. Criminals as young as sixteen years of age were still being sentenced to transportation to Australasia. The poor agricultural classes were the one social section of society that were unable to benefit from the advances in the standards of living. This was reflected in the many instances of sudden deaths within the poorest sections of society.

1845 was yet another year that exemplified the many varied and unusual modes of sudden death in the county. Children were still being burnt to death and were drowning in ponds, even if they stayed clear of the myriad diseases that threatened society. Men found ways of being crushed, dismembered, drowned or suffocated during the course of their working lives. Newspapers had all the material they required to continue titillating their readership with the dreadful stories of misfortune suffered predominantly by the working classes.

The first notable report from January 1845 concerned another poor family and another 'burnt child'.

> Before Mr. Wood, on Tuesday last, at Woodbridge, on Thema Suggate, aged 7 years, daughter of John Suggate, brickmaker. It appeared that this family are all very poor, and the mother went on Saturday last to Great Bealings for "a gift of coals," leaving this poor girl and several other children in her own cottage *without any fire*. They, however, went during her absence, into a neighbour's house who had left a fire there. By some accident the clothes of Thema ignited; she ran out immediately into the yard, when she met Robert Green, a young sailor, who rolled her in the snow and then covered her with water. Medical assistance was immediately resorted to; but she was too much burnt to recover, and died on Monday evening. Verdict, "Accidentally burnt." The Jury did not cast any blame on the mother.

Another death at the beginning of the year concerned the body of a baby discovered in a ditch at Sutton.

> On the 31st Dec last, as two boys were throwing stones at some birds near a plantation belonging to Robert Knipe Cobbold, Esq., in Sutton, called "Hulver Plantation," they found in a ditch, near the public path leading from Woodbridge Ferry to Sutton church, the dead body of a child wrapped up in a woman's apron. They immediately

gave information to the parish constable, who took charge of it, and on the 2nd of January an inquest upon the body of this child was held by Mr. Wood. Mr. Kett, surgeon, deposed that from the state of decomposition of the body, it was impossible to state whether the child had been born alive or not, and if it was, how it came by its death; he was satisfied it was a female. The apron was delivered to the police, and the inquest adjourned until Monday last, the 20th inst., to give time for further inquiries. The Jury accordingly re-assembled on that day, but as nothing farther had, in the meantime, been discovered, the Jury returned a verdict of "Found Dead." It is a common apron and no mark of any kind is upon it, so that this affair will probably remain forever a mystery.

An unsolved mystery. By now, there were groups of unexplained deaths appearing in the columns of the local press. For example in mid-March there were four deaths reported - a seven week old baby boy who died in bed next to his mother, a 57 year old former shoemaker of Parham who died in his sleep, an old woman, Lucy Smith, of Framlingham, who "was burnt to death in her own cottage" and another infant, who from the evidence appeared to have been neglected from birth. Later that month there was a rather fanciful conclusion to a woman's premature and somewhat mysterious death.

On Thursday last at Ringshall, on view of the body of Mrs. Keziah Durrant, aged 28, wife of Mr. James Durrant of Finborough. The deceased, who was on a visit to her father, and who was in apparent good health, and had been busily engaged during the morning, went upstairs about 2 o'clock on Tuesday last, to change her dress, and remaining a considerable time, she was found upon her knees at the foot of the bed quite dead, and from her position it was evident that the vital spark had fled whilst she was engaged in prayer. Verdict: "Died by the Visitation of God."

We move on to June 1845 and another paragraph of inquest reports, complete with many of the lurid details.

On Wednesday at Rendham, upon the body Elizabeth Pendle, widow, and for more than 20 years a faithful servant of Miss Williams of that parish. Mrs. Pendle had been for several years subject to rheumatism, but had otherwise enjoyed good health. On Tuesday last she was employed in baking, and about 12 o'clock suddenly fell down, and expired in three or four minutes. Verdict, "Died by the Visitation of God."

On Thursday, at Debenham, upon the body of Sutton Ludbrook, aged 3 years, (son of James Ludbrook, of the same place, shoemaker), who was found drowned in the Deben about two o'clock the preceding afternoon. This child was in the daily habit of playing near a foot bridge across the river, and it is supposed he fell off the bridge, he having been seen nearby, about half an hour before. Verdict, "Accidentally drowned."

The same evening, at Sudbourne, on the body of Sarah Cook, aged 41 years, the wife of Charles Cook, of that parish, labourer. Until Tuesday afternoon, Mrs. Cook had enjoyed good health, and was the mother of six children.

About 4 o'clock on Wednesday morning, her husband went to Orford for medical assistance; she was attended by a surgeon and bled. A neighbour, on being requested, promised to attend her; but having care of some children, and not being aware of Mrs. Cook's dangerous state, left the cottage for a short time. Another visitor went in and found her a corpse. Verdict, "Visitation of God." It was previously reported that the deceased had been neglected, but there was no evidence given upon the inquest as any foundation for such a report.

In July 1845, another young man fell under the wheels of his fully-loaded waggon in Earl Soham and a young boy had the misfortune to be kicked by a horse in the parish of Brandeston.

On Thursday last, at Earl Soham, on the body of Charles Gilbert, aged 23, servant to Mr. Bigsby, of the same place. It appeared that Gilbert was returning to Earl Soham, with a waggon-load of ling, drawn by four horses, and seen to pass through the village about 2 o'clock. In a few minutes afterwards, he was found in the road quite dead, and from the situation of the body, it appeared that the near wheels of the waggon had passed over him. Verdict, "Accidental death." Gilbert was a single man and sober at the time.

On Saturday last, at Brandeston, on the body of Dennis Moore, aged 12 years. From the evidence it appeared that this boy was on Monday, the 23rd of June, employed by William Barber, of Kettleburgh, labourer, to tread some clay, and when he had finished, to scrape the legs of the horse; in doing this the horse, with one of his hind legs, struck Dennis Moore on the lower part of his body. Barber, who was present, immediately picked him up, and although complaining of great pain Barber went nowhere for assistance, but after laying him down in different places, made the boy walk home, a distance of two miles. His father immediately sent for a medical man, when it turned out to be a bad case, and after lingering until Friday morning, Moore died. Verdict "Accidental Death," with a deodand of one shilling upon the horse. The Coroner, at the request of the Jury, severely reprimanded Barber for his want of humanity, although there was from the first but little chance of saving the poor boy's life.

A melancholy drowning accident occurred in August.

On Saturday August the 26th, an inquest was held at the Magpie Inn, Harleston, Norfolk, before John Musket, Esq., Coroner, and a very respectable jury, upon the body of Charles Riches, of Mendham, labourer, a fine good looking young man, of the age of 25 years, who came by his death on the previous evening, under the following circumstances. It appeared that he went to the river Waveney, below Shotford Hall, for the purpose of teaching his master's brother (Mr. Broughton) to swim, the deceased being an excellent swimmer. After he had been in the water a few minutes, he was observed suddenly to sink, wringing his hands, and although a rope was thrown to him directly, he did not appear to take the least notice of it, but immediately sank to rise no more. The poor fellow was married but a week ago, and his widow is plunged into the deepest distress. Verdict - "Accidental death."

In September, a case of arsenic poisoning came to the attention of the Coroner.

On Saturday last, at Bruisyard, on the body of Emma Aldridge, aged 20 years, servant to Samuel Greenard, of the same place, farmer. The first witness was Dr. Lay, of Peasenhall, who attended her the previous day for about an hour, when suffering most dreadfully from the effects of a large quantity of arsenic she had swallowed, and was present at her death; he afterwards made a post mortem examination of the body, with an analysis of the contents of the stomach, and was quite certain that she died from the effects of the poison. It also appeared in evidence that she had, late on Thursday evening, purchased two pennyworth of arsenic at a shop in Peasenhall (where she had been well known for nearly two years) in the name of her mistress for the purpose of destroying mice, with which she stated the house was overrun. Her master and mistress (to whom she acknowledged having taken the arsenic), and two fellow servants were also examined, when it appeared, and the fact was confirmed by the Doctor, that she was in a very advanced state of pregnancy. Not the slightest alteration had been observed in her manner or conduct until she became affected by the poison, and no act of lunacy having been proved, the Jury (13 out of 17) immediately returned a verdict of "Felo-de-se," and she was, under the Coroner's order, buried in Bruisyard churchyard the same evening of the inquest, without any funeral rites. The enquiry lasted between 5 and 6 hours.

October brought another round of sudden deaths and inquests across the county.

On the 20th instant at the Crown Inn, Woolpit, on the body of David Nunn, a gardener, between 50 and 60 years of age, who on the previous evening, about 8 o'clock, was so intoxicated that he reeled into the road against the shaft of a cart and fell violently to the ground and was run over. Mr. Slayter, surgeon, considered that death arose from concussion of the brain, occasioned by the fall on his head; and the witness who saw the accident acquitted the driver of the cart of all blame. Verdict - "Accidental death."

On Tuesday last, at Framlingham, on the body of Benjamin Goodwin, aged 75 years. Goodwin had formerly been a soldier, but latterly followed his trade of a shoemaker; earning however a sad pittance, he received a weekly allowance from the parish, and lived in a small cottage with James Taveyear, who went out to work early on Monday morning, leaving Goodwin in bed well. Returning at 6 o'clock, p.m., he found Goodwin dead in his bed; he had been seen by several persons during the day; about three o'clock he asked change for a sixpence. Verdict "Natural death." Goodwin had never been married, and left not a single relative.

Same evening, at Rendham, on the body of David Barker, aged 23 months, son of Samuel Barker, labourer. It appeared that Mrs. Barker had been baking on Saturday, and his grandmother had been taking off the fire a kettle of boiling water, which she had placed on the backhouse floor.

She was called away hastily and on her return in two minutes, found that the kettle had been overturned and the child sodden with the hot water. Upon stripping him immediately it was ascertained he had been dreadfully scalded on the chest and body from which he lingered until Monday afternoon, when he died. Verdict, "Accidental Death."

On Monday last, at Sudbourne, on the body of Mary Ann Day, (the illegitimate child of Mary Ann Day, of that parish, single woman) aged 4 weeks. It appeared in evidence that this child was born in the Plomesgate Union House at Wickham Market, which the mother quitted at her own desire at the end of 3 weeks. That the child had been very sickly from its birth and on Wednesday the 3rd inst. was found dead in bed by its mother. In consequence of some demur about registering its death, the parish officers decided upon having an enquiry before a jury, who returned a unanimous verdict of "Natural Death."

We bring the curtain down on 1845 with yet another occurrence of accidental burning.

On Thursday, at Campsey Ash, on the body of Jeremiah Pratt, (son of Jeremiah Pratt, of that parish, labourer) aged 4 years. From the evidence it appeared that on the 21st November, about noon time, the mother left the back door of her cottage open to feed a neighbour's pigs, and very soon afterwards heard this boy shrieking violently. On returning to the house, she found him enveloped in flames, which, with the assistance of a neighbour, were soon extinguished.

The child had proper medical and other attention but died on Wednesday morning. Verdict, "Accidentally burnt."

Reports in 1846 demonstrate again the range of sudden deaths occurring in Suffolk in the middle of the 19th century. The first month set the tone for the rest of the year with numerous cases keeping the Coroner and his assistant busy. Reporting was relatively sparse in the details given; column inches must have been at a premium. The Ipswich Journal was still just a eight page newspaper.

On Friday, the 26th of December last, at Martlesham, on the body of David Grayston, of Clopton, aged 45 years, who was accidentally killed whilst in a state of intoxication, by the upsetting of his cart, on the Wednesday preceding. Verdict - "Accidental Death."

On the following day at Rendlesham on the body of Samuel Ling, aged 71 years, who was found dead that morning in a road leading from Tunstall to Woodbridge. Verdict - "Died from the inclemency of the weather."

On Tuesday last, at Framsden, on the body of Samuel Oxborrow, aged 55 years, who was found by his wife the Sunday morning preceding, suspended by a handkerchief to the bed-post. Verdict - "Temporary Insanity."

On Wednesday at Ramsholt, on the body of John Hayes, aged 26 years, who received a kick on the lower part of his body from one of two horses he was driving in a Chicory engine, the previous day. Verdict - "Accidental Death."

On Thursday evening at Melton, on the body of William Chaplin, aged 5 years, who was so much burnt the day before, in the temporary absence of his mother, that he survived only 15 hours. Verdict - "Accidentally burnt to death."

On Friday the 30th ult., at Bredfield, on the body of William Clarke, a respectable carpenter in that parish, who early that morning was returning with his son from Mr. T. Grimwood's annual frolic at Woodbridge, and it being extremely dark, accidentally fell upon his face into a deep miry ditch, adjoining the road in that parish. His son being unable to extricate him obtained immediately the assistance of two other men, but when Clarke was taken out, he was dead. Verdict - "Accidental death from suffocation."

On rare occasions, a simply bizarre report really raised the eyebrows, as this one must have done in April 1846.

On Tuesday morning last Mr. Wood held an inquest at Great Bealings, upon the body of William Lewis, a boy aged 12 years, who met his death in the following extraordinary manner. Lewis had been for a considerable time in the employ of Mr. Brundley, and his duty was to fetch up the cows night and morning. On Monday afternoon, when driving home the cows, he tied the tail of one round his body, and it is supposed she became frightened, as she was seen running past some houses dragging the poor boy upon the hard road, and kicking him at intervals most violently; after dragging him thus upwards of 100 yards and through the river, he became disengaged, and when picked up by two men who followed the cow, he groaned a little but expired on his way to his master's house, his skull having been fractured in a most shocking manner. Verdict, "Accidental Death." Lewis was a very quiet harmless boy, and much respected by his master.

The weather also took its toll on those who toiled in the fields, as in this case reported during the same month.

An inquest was held on Friday last, in this town (Bury St. Edmunds) on the body of Isaac Bryant, aged 19, whose death took place the previous day under the circumstances stated in the following evidence.

Charles Goddard of Well Street, Bury stated: "I was at wheat-hoeing in a field at Westley, in the occupation of the Marquis of Bristol; the deceased and six other lads were with me. Soon after two o'clock in consequence of a heavy cloud coming over us, we all made to the fence for shelter. We had been there about ten minutes when a strong flash of lightning came. I was standing a few yards off the rest, and putting a stone bottle to my mouth at the time. It was knocked out of my hand. Six of the lads came shrieking to me immediately, and as soon as we had recovered ourselves we went to the spot where they had stood and found Isaac Bryant had fallen down with his head a little under the bushes. His trousers from a little above the knee to a little beneath it were in flames. I nipped them out with my hands, and looking at his face thought it showed slight symptoms of life, but I don't think he lived scarcely a minute afterwards. On the right temple was the appearance as if a hot iron had been struck across it; the hair was a little singed, and the flesh appeared as if it had been scorched. It is a high thick clipped hedge with two trees in it where the lads stood."

William Bryant, brother of the deceased, deposed that he was sitting on a basket under the hedge when his brother was struck, who was standing by at the time, with his hoe under his arm and his hand in his pocket. Three lads were sitting down and three were standing up. James Bryant, another brother, deposed that he was knocked away from the hedge by the flash, but did not fall. He was also burnt between the legs at the inner part of the knee of the left leg.

Mr. Peachey, surgeon, of Risbygate Street, detailed the appearances presented by the body. It appeared as if a considerable quantity of the fluid was concentrated under the deceased's person; the hoe, which was bright, might have acted as a conductor. Verdict, "Died by the Visitation of God."

This last paragraph of the report summarising the surgeon's observations illustrates the prevailing concept of electricity at that time. It was then no more than a scientific curiosity. The term "fluid" referred to the electric strike of the lightning bolt, though the use of the word "conductor" suggests a knowledge of the principles of the lightning phenomenon by the surgeon. However, the verdict signifying the will of God being involved once again prolonged the myth to the labouring classes that mighty forces were at work directing their lives from above.

As we have already seen, accidents and sudden deaths involving modes of transport were quite common, whether by road transport, rail transport or by ship.

On Thursday last, at the Steam Packet public-house, in the parish of St. Clement, Ipswich, on the body of William Wade, aged 17, apprentice on board the brig Orwell, the property of John Cobbold, Esq. About three o'clock on Wednesday afternoon, after passing over a plank which extended from the quay, and rested on the hatches, the deceased's foot slipped accidentally, and he fell into the hold, making a descent of about seventeen feet. The mate, Stephen Argent, was in the hold at the time, and in attempting to catch the deceased, was injured on the right side of the head, from which blood flowed profusely for some time afterwards.

The poor boy was removed to his home, and had the assistance of Mr. Bartlett, surgeon, but he was so severely injured by the fall, that he never rallied, and died about five o'clock. Verdict, "Accidental death from an injury on the left side of the head, by a fall on the bottom of the hold of the brig Orwell." The deceased was spoken of as a very steady, industrious and promising lad, having always borne an excellent character.

Deaths were meticulously recorded and reported in the newspapers, such were the curious methods by which the inhabitants of the county unexpectedly expired.

At Assington, on the body of Nathan Ward, who being engaged in rook-taking, fell from a height of near 50 feet by the breaking of the bough on which he was, and broke his neck. Verdict, "Accidental Death."

At Acton, on the body of James Upson, aged 27 years, jobber, a single man, who broke a blood-vessel on his lungs on Saturday night, just after leaving the Crown Inn, being of a consumptive habit, and died almost immediately. Verdict accordingly.

On Wednesday last, at Barking, on view of the body of James Mullett, a child of the age of 8 years, who met his death in the following manner. The child was playing in the road near Barking Tye, when another boy only twelve years old came up, who was driving a horse in a tumbrel, to which was affixed a roll; the deceased got on to the roll for a ride and suddenly falling off it, the roll passed over his head and body. The child was picked up bleeding profusely from the mouth and nose, and died before he could be got home. Verdict, "Accidental Death."

At Halesworth, on Tuesday last, on the body of William More, aged 72, who on the Friday before, was found dead. It appeared that the deceased had been on a visit to his nephew and had walked out after breakfast intending to return to dinner, but not making his appearance at the time he was expected, a search was made, when he was found dead in a ditch containing about two feet of water, into which it was supposed he had fallen. Verdict - "Found Dead."

On the 5th inst., at Tostock, on the body of Rachael Hinnell, aged 46, for ten years housekeeper to the Rev. James Oakes, who having received warning from her master the previous day, at a time when she was suffering from depression occasioned by her fears that an abscess in the palm of her hand would never heal, drowned herself in the fish pond. Verdict, "Temporary Insanity."

On the 6th at Tostock, on the body of Charles Wilden, aged 18, labourer on the railway, who, in unhooking the tip chain, caught his neck in the chain, so that his head went between the bumpers of the waggons and was crushed to pieces. He died almost instantly. Verdict, "Accidental Death," deodand 1s.

In July 1846, an awful tragedy occurred in Kelsale. We cannot imagine the horrified state of the poor woman who witnessed the shocking act of self-destruction. The reader will take note of the relative ordinariness of the subsequent reports printed in the newspaper.

On Wednesday last, at Kelsale, on the body of George Self, a labourer. Last Tuesday, the deceased went into a field with Mrs. Low, a neighbour, taking a gun for the purpose of shooting sparrows, which was afterwards charged - whilst Mrs. Low was looking away from him, the deceased placed the barrel of the gun in his mouth and fired it off, thereby mutilating his head in a dreadful manner; he died instantly. It appeared that the deceased had for some time been in a desponding state of mind, proceeding from the effects of a fever, and the loss of his little savings, which had compelled him much against his inclination, to apply for parish relief; and that he had on previous occasions made attempts on his life. Verdict - "Shot himself whilst in a deranged state of mind."

At Charsfield, on the 29th ult., on the body of Emma Leech, single woman, aged 20 years, who died early on the preceding Sunday morning, after vomiting for several hours. The Coroner directed a post mortem examination, by which it was ascertained she was 6 months advanced in pregnancy, and was suspected to have died from the effects of some poison. In order, therefore, to give the medical man (Mr. Jones) sufficient time to have the small quantity of fluid found in the stomach properly analysed, the inquest was adjourned until the following Friday.

On the Jury re-assembling, Mr. Jones deposed that he had (assisted by several eminent chemists) analysed the contents of the stomach, but had not been able to find any poisonous matter, which he accounted for from her having been vomiting for several hours before her death, as proved by the first witness called. The Jury therefore returned a verdict of "Natural Death."

On the 30th ult., at Farnham, on the body of John Everitt, labourer, aged 73, who hanged himself that morning in a stable belonging to Mr. Stephen Gooding. It having been proved that Everitt had been for some time in a low melancholy way, the Jury returned a verdict of "Lunacy."

On the 25th ult., at the Bushel Inn, in the borough of Bury St. Edmunds, on the body of Sarah Corne, aged 82, who on the previous day, missed her step when crossing the road to her home in the Long Blackland, and fell backwards just as a cart, driven by James Frost, was coming along, the wheel of which went over her chest and killed her almost upon the spot. The poor old woman was in the receipt of poor relief and increased the scanty pittance by selling nets etc. in the market. Verdict - "Accidental Death."

The following case from August 1846 highlighted the lengths to which the poor had to go to earn enough money to survive, when the sickly young woman still went out gleaning. The living conditions that the poor had to endure are also noted.

On the 5th inst., at Newbourne, on the body of Elizabeth Ely, aged 23, who had been in a sickly state of health for several years, but was out gleaning all Tuesday, supped with her father and brother, and went to bed before ten o'clock. About 2 the following morning, her father, who slept in the same room, was awakened by a strange noise she was making in her throat; he got up directly and found her insensible; he called for assistance to his neighbour living under the same roof, but before anyone could arrive, she was dead. The verdict given was - "Died by the Visitation of God."

In September 1846, a riding accident occurred at Sutton and another case of a child burnt to death was investigated at Wickham Market.

On Monday last, at Sutton, on the body of John Pooley, aged 13 years. It was proved by his elder brother that very early on Wednesday morning, they fetched up Mr. Edwards's horses from the marshes and that John was riding upon one of the mares but had not buckled the throat-latch of the dutfin. In attempting to stop the mare when going at a full trot, the dutfin came off and John Pooley falling under the feet of the mare, she set one foot upon his body. He was carried home and lingered in great agony until Saturday night when death put an end to his sufferings. Verdict - "Accidental Death." This mare would have become a deodand had not the Act of Parliament abolishing deodands come into operation on the 1st.

On September 18th, at Wickham Market, on the body of Spencer Winter, a child under 3 years of age. On the Tuesday night previous, his mother had taken him upstairs to bed and left him, while she went down to fetch some water. His sudden screams recalled her, and on returning upstairs found him dreadfully burnt. He lingered until the following night, when death relieved him of his sufferings. Verdict - "Death from accidental burning."

In November, there was another case of infant sudden death through burning. In this case, the child must have suffered excruciating pain for nearly 24 hours. A further inquest that month blamed ferrets for causing a riding accident resulting in the death of the rider. Further inquest reports from that month are also reproduced.

On the 2nd inst., at Kenton, on the body of Caleb Boon, aged 4 years. The child had been left in the care of his grandmother, and crossed the road to play with some other children in the cottage of Robert Smith, where his clothes caught fire, and he was so much burned that he died from the effects thereof in about 24 hours. Verdict "Death from accidental burning."

On Wednesday morning last, at Hollesley, on the body of James Fleming, coachman and groom to the Misses Felgate, of Bawdsey. About four o'clock the preceding afternoon, Fleming was riding a young mare towards Hollesley street. In about 5 minutes afterwards the mare was seen to return without her rider; search was immediately made and Fleming was found dead in the road with his neck broken. A bag containing three live ferrets was found in his pocket, and it is supposed that the mare taking fright from their movements suddenly plunged and threw Fleming off. Verdict, "Accidental death."

Same evening, at Trimley Mariners, on the body of Eliza Jane Churchman, aged 13 months, youngest child of Mr. Wm. Churchman, of Trimley St. Martin. From the evidence of Emma Rush, the servant girl, it appeared that this child was healthy, but was not well when put to bed on Tuesday evening: that she was very restless during the night, and was found dead about six o'clock on Wednesday morning.

Same evening, at Hoo, by Mr. John Richard Wood, Deputy Coroner, on the body of Martha Fryett, a poor widow, aged 49 years. It appeared in evidence that she had been subject to fits. Upon getting up about seven that morning she was visited with one of her attacks, and died instantly. Her mother died in a similar way some years back. The Jurors verdicts in the last two cases "Death by the Visitation of God."

On the 20th inst., at Bawdsey, on Rose Ann Sare, aged 9 years. It appeared by the evidence that this little girl was on the preceding afternoon on Bawdsey Beach, picking up shells, when a part of the cliff fell down and buried her. An alarm was given by two young women who were also on the beach, and her father and three other men came and extricated her in half an hour, but life was extinct. Verdict - "Accidental death."

Finally in December 1846, a report of a death which brought into focus again the use of the verdict "Visitation of God", used when there appeared to be a sudden, unexplained natural death.

On Saturday last, Mr. John Wood jun., Coroner for the Liberty of St. Etheldred, held an inquest at Wantisden, on the body of Samuel Richardson, aged 78 years, who died suddenly the previous day. The deceased had walked to Butley, about a mile distant, to receive his parochial relief, and on his return sat down to supper, after which he went to bed apparently as well as usual; however, in about a quarter of an hour, he complained to his wife and son of a pain in his chest, and his wife made him a cup of tea, thinking it might relieve him of the pain he suffered; he drank the tea, but in about half an hour he expired. Verdict - "Natural Death by the Visitation of God."

Before looking at the sudden deaths that were reported in the newspapers of 1847, we can reflect on the previous year and list a few of the bizarre and tragic ways that people had their lives ended.

Fell off a cart whilst intoxicated
Died from the inclemency of the weather
Hung himself from the bedpost
Kicked by a horse
Burnt to death
Attached to a cow tail
Hung himself in a stable
Run over by a cart wheel
Buried by a cliff
Death by the Visitation of God

1847 was what could only be described as another typical year for sudden deaths and January featured two of the commonest means

On Thursday last, at Woodbridge, before Mr. Wood, on the body of Margaret Copping, widow, aged 76 years. Mrs. Copping had for the last twelve months been lodging at the house of Mr. James Nunn, brazier, having the sole use of the first floor; it was her practice to drink tea every evening about 7 o'clock, and afterwards to wash up her tea things. On Tuesday evening at about 8 o'clock she was heard to scream violently, and was found literally enveloped in flames; several persons came to her immediate assistance, and she was speedily attended by two medical men, but she died about 12 o'clock the following day. It is supposed that she was standing with her back too near the fire, when her clothes ignited. Verdict - "Accidentally burnt."

Martlesham Red Lion

On Saturday last, at Martlesham, on the body of Frederick Robinson, aged one year and three-quarters, who was scalded on Monday the 4th inst., by the accidental upsetting of a kettle of boiling water. The poor little fellow lingered in great agony until Friday 8th when death put an end to his sufferings. Verdict - "Accidental death."

Natural death and a drowning were amongst a large number of sudden deaths in the columns of the January newspapers. In the case of Phebe Burton, we also read of the growing concern expressed by the newspaper of the inadequate measures to protect children from being burnt to death.

On Monday last, at Earl Soham, on the body of Thomas Thrower, aged 71, who was found dead in bed on the night of the 8th inst. He had been unwell for a few days, and had some medicine given him on the 6th by Mr. Gross, surgeon, of Earl Soham, very little of which he had taken, and his family had culpably neglected to send for Mr. Gross. The jury, however, feeling satisfied that he died by the visitation of God, returned a verdict to that effect.

On the 24th inst., at Freckenham, on the body of Charles Chittock, aged 46, a pauper of weak intellects, who, on the previous night, having first called out to his sister that he wanted to go out, as he frequently had occasion to do, went out by the wrong door, and was found the next morning lying entirely naked and quite dead in a field about 200 yards away, with every appearance of having been through the pond. Mr. Aldrich, of Mildenhall, said the deceased was of weak intellect, and laboured under an affliction of the spine, affecting the lower extremities, and that death had been occasioned by exposure to the inclemency of the weather. Verdict accordingly.

On the 26th inst., at Haverhill, on the body of Eliza Nunn, aged 4½ years, who in attempting to climb up the back of a chair, fell down with it, and hitting the back of her head, dislocated her neck and died instantly. Verdict - "Accidental Death."

On the 28th inst., at the Suffolk General Hospital, on the body of Phebe Burton, aged 12, "short-sighted and of weak intellect," who having been left on the 18th inst., by her mother at No. 104, Short Brackland, to undress by the fire, set fire to her things in getting a ball of cotton from the mantel-piece, and was so burnt as to be obliged to be removed to the Hospital, where she died on the 27th. Verdict accordingly. The use of a fire guard would have prevented this painful occurrence. We have before recommended these guards as suitable winter presents to the poor, whose occupations prevent them, in many cases, from attending properly to their children. The subject is one of great importance, for the deaths arising from this cause alone, during the winter months, make a very considerable item in the general amount of mortality.

On January 30th, at Walton, on the body of Lavinia Mary Warner, aged 4 years, daughter of Charles Warner, of the same place, miller. It was proved by two witnesses that on the afternoon of Tuesday the 26th that the child, who was in perfect health, was going home from school, when William James Catt, a boy under seven years of age, came up and struck her a violent blow on the body with his fist. She was immediately taken ill and got worse until noontime the following Thursday when she died. Mr. Wilkin saw and prescribed for the little girl on the Wednesday morning, but was not again sent for. He was examined on the inquest, but the jury did not then think it necessary to have a post mortem examination. Catt was brought before the jury and acknowledged having struck the blow, but said she had a short time before slapped his face. Jurors' verdict - "Homicide by the said William James Catt, then and there being an infant under the age of discretion."

In February 1847, it was Mother Nature who bestowed a premature death on an old labourer, who it appeared stood petrified by fear.

> On Tuesday last, at Ufford, on the body of Robert Balls, aged 60 years, who came by his death in the following melancholy manner. It appears that the deceased was employed tying up the faggot wood from some trees that were felled near Ufford Lion, and whilst so doing, another tree fell upon him, and killed him on the spot. Several men who were there called out to him to get out of the way while the tree was falling, but he appeared frightened, and as if he did not know which way to go. Not the slightest blame can be attached to anyone, as he could see the tree was falling. Verdict - "Accidental death."

In early March, we have a sudden death and inquest that did not reach the local newspapers. This was another case of a child burnt to death, though the accident occurred outside of the family home. David Smith, who worked as a brick-maker for the girl's father, gave the following evidence under oath:

> "I know Edward Boon and Caroline his wife, the parents of the said Ann Boon and have done so about three years. They had four children before Ann died; she was the youngest. I worked for Edward Boon and have done so all the time I have known him. I knew the little girl Ann Boon very well. I saw her very often. I saw her on Saturday last the sixth day of March, about a quarter before two o'clock in the afternoon. She was then in perfect health. She was playing in the brickyard not above half a rod off the brick kiln; the

bricks were all red hot and the heat steaming out. Jane Boon, another little girl a little older than Ann, was with her and about a quarter of an hour after I last saw Ann alive and well, I heard Jane screaming out that her sister was on fire. I ran directly and saw her clothes on fire; she was standing on the side of the kiln and her clothes blazing up above her head. There was no one there except her little brother, a little older than Jane. I put the fire out as well as I could and gave Ann, who was burnt on her face and throat, to Job Pipe, a man who was also working in the yard. Pipe took off her things and carried her into her father's house.

Mr. Wilson, a surgeon, was sent for directly and he came in about half an hour but the said Ann Boon died about nine o'clock on Sunday night. I have no doubt but she died in consequence of this burning, which I know was accidental by her going too near the hot bricks."

The verdict returned by the jury was "Death by accidental burning."

Industrial accidents came to the fore in April 1847 with two young men coming by their deaths in the most unfortunate circumstances.

On Thursday last, at the White Horse, Brandon, on the body of Charles Rampling, labourer, who met his death in a most unfortunate manner, on Tuesday last, while at work in a well belonging to the Rev. Mr. Cartwright. The deceased had been at the bottom of the well, which was 20 feet deep, levelling the kerb preparatory to the brick work being commenced, when the earth caved in from the middle of the well, filling it up about 10 feet. On being taken out, three hours after, he was found to be quite dead. Verdict - "Accidental death."

On Saturday last, at the Victoria Inn, Berners Street, on the body of Michael Terry, who came by his death in the following manner. That morning, between 8 and 9 o'clock, the deceased was employed in unloading two railway waggons, near the Griffin Inn. Whilst in the act of pushing an oak tree from one of the waggons into the river, three trees slipped off the waggon on the opposite side. The deceased, who was upon the topmost tree, fell head first upon the road, and before he could get out of the way, one of the trees fell upon his head, which was crushed in a shocking manner. He was heard to exclaim, "Oh Lord have mercy upon me!" He never spoke again, and died on his way to the hospital. The Jury returned a verdict of "Accidental death." The unfortunate man, who was 31 years of age, has left a widow and child.

In November 1847, a young boy of tender years, employed in the railway marshalling yards at Ipswich, suffered briefly in a most horrendous accident. How could a 14 year old boy be "equal to the work in which he had been engaged?"

An inquest was held on Tuesday last, at the Lion public house, St. Mary Stoke, on the body of David Garwood, 14 years of age. It appeared from the evidence of John Cobbold, a railway labourer, that the deceased was at work on the new tramway leading towards the Wet Dock, near to the "Black Bridge," which spans the river Gipping. He was employed to apply the break to the waggons laden with earth, and on the afternoon of Monday, when five earth waggons were descending the incline over the bridge, the deceased was seen to insert the break-pole in the off wheel of the first waggon, but owing to the slippery state of the pole, from the wet and dirt upon it, it slipped out of the wheel, causing the deceased to be thrown across the rail; when the wheels of the second and third waggons passed over his belly and loins. A man present snatched the body of the deceased from off the rail, thus preventing the wheels of the fourth waggon passing over the body. The poor little fellow breathed twice, and then expired; his body doubled up when removed from under the waggons, as if his back was broken. It having been stated by two witnesses that the deceased was equal to the work in which he had been engaged, and that the cause of the deceased's death was entirely the result of an accident, the jury returned a verdict of "Accidental death."

During the same month, an unfortunate case of suicide occurred at Rattlesden.

On Friday morning, November 26th, the friends of Mr. Robert Winson, miller, of Rattlesden, were horror-struck at learning that he had committed suicide by hanging himself. The unfortunate man was found suspended by the neck in the upper floor of the new mill, and when discovered was quite dead. The deceased was at Stowmarket on the day previous, and appeared in his usual health and spirits, and on the morning of the melancholy act had written a note to the station-master at Stowmarket, and dispatched it by one of his men with a load of flour to be conveyed by train to London.

At the inquest, before H. Wayman, Gent., the Coroner, on Saturday, Mr. Robert Winson deposed that he had seen his father, who was 48 years of age, very low spirited at times, especially since he met with an accident by part of a building falling upon him; and at times he was neglectful and forgetful of his business. Mr. Growse, surgeon, who had attended the deceased for 25 years, said that, some months ago, he met with an accident, producing concussion of the brain and fracture of the shoulder-joint, and that since then he had seen a marked alteration in the state of his mind. Verdict "Temporary Insanity."

Amongst a plethora of inquests in December 1847, there were examples of more accidents at work.

On Monday 6th last, on the body of Michael O'Brien, aged 50, who was found dead - partly in a pond - at Rendham on Sunday morning. It appeared that deceased was a travelling spectacle seller, and that he was the worse for liquor on Saturday night. He left two companions on the road for Saxmundham, and expressed his determination to go by the fields. He was found the next morning lying with his head in the pond, but with no marks of violence on his body, and 11s 9d in his pockets. The presumption therefore is that he fell in and was unable to get out again. Verdict "Found drowned."

On the 11th inst., at the Bell Inn, Great Wratting, on the body of Robert Bowers, aged 2 years. The mother, Elizabeth Bowers, deposed to having on the previous day left the three youngest of her children (the eldest of her family of four was only 7 years old,) alone in her house, there being at the time a very little fire. On returning about twenty minutes after, upon opening the door of her room, she found it full of smoke. She then went to the cradle and took her infant out and set him out abroad; she then went again into the house and saw the deceased with the lower part of his clothes up to the waist burnt off, and himself very much burnt. He died about four o'clock the following morning. Verdict "Accidentally burned."

When will mothers take the warning not to leave their infant children alone in a room with fire? Twenty short minutes in this instance, suffice to destroy one life, and embitter the recollection of another; and it might be supposed that the numerous cases which happen of the same sort, would lead others to guard against such careless neglect. (editorial comment)

On Monday 13th at the Safe Harbour Inn, Ipswich, on the body of Hannah Ribbans, aged 77, who that morning was found dead in her bed. It appeared that she had for some time suffered from a cough, but on the previous night went to bed apparently well as usual. According to one of the witnesses, she was "on the parish, but had good friends." Verdict "Pulmonary apoplexy."

The Ship Inn, Ipswich circa 1912

At the Ship Inn on Tuesday 14th, on the body of Henry Maple, aged 30. It appeared that the deceased was a working engineer employed at Mr. Tovell's steam engine, for grinding cement. On the previous day he was so crushed by the fly wheel, as to occasion his death before arriving at the East Suffolk Hospital. The deceased was represented to be a sober and steady man, and an accidental slip from a plank was supposed to have been the cause of the catastrophe. Verdict "Accidental death." The deceased has left a wife and two children.

On Friday, the 17th, at the Star Commercial Hotel, Lowestoft, on the body of Walter Riches aged 27. It appeared that the deceased and Thos. Smith were employed in digging a well on the premises of the late Mr. Everard. From the influx of water, when they had attained a depth of 32 feet, the sand was so acted upon, as to cave in, and both the men were entirely buried. A man named Henry Rose, of Lowestoft, was passing when the accident occurred. He saw the confusion near the wheel, and was informed that two men were buried in the well. Finding that the men standing about were afraid of going down, he determined to descend himself. The result was that he found Smith, covered by earth up to the mouth. Having cleared the soil away as far as he could, he asked Smith where his fellow labourer was. Smith replied he was underneath, when Rose succeeded in getting hold of the deceased's hand; he found, however, that the earth kept falling in as quickly as it was removed, and his own life being in danger he came up again, Smith telling him not to remove any more sand.

John Newson, a bricklayer, then procured some iron hoops, and went down, as no one else would go. After three hours hard labour, he succeeded in extricating Smith and got him up; Riches, he discovered to be quite dead. In answer to several questions it appeared that Mr. Cooper, the master of the work, was at Kirkley at the time of the accident, but arrived at the spot about an hour after Newson went down. It was also shown that the deceased and his companion had been accustomed to digging wells in Cley, in Norfolk, where the earth is composed of clay or chalk, and that in digging the well in question they had not taken the necessary precautions to protect themselves from the loose sand.

Mr. Worthington, the surgeon, examined the body when it was brought up, and ordered it to be removed to the Infirmary, where he used every means to resuscitate the body, but without effect. There did not appear to have been any bones broken, and it was Mr. Worthington's opinion that the deceased died from suffocation. The Coroner summed up the evidence, and the jury found a verdict of "Accidental death," accompanied by a strong expression of their approbation of the highly meritorious conduct of the two witnesses, Henry Rose and John Newson; and expressing a wish that some means should be devised to reward them for their humane exertions.

So ended the almost interminable list of sudden deaths and inquests in 1847, many of which were reported in the columns of the Ipswich Journal. The 1848 newspaper columns were unlikely to be any less populated with stories of misery and misfortune, as we shall learn.

9

1848-1849 - How on earth could this HAPPEN?

Parts of this chapter are devoted to asking how certain situations were allowed to develop and accidents allowed to happen. For example, in early January 1848, a fatal accident occurred in the barn of the Red House farm at Bawdsey.

Threshing machines were gradually replacing the old way of threshing with the flail, reducing the amount of time needed to separate the grain from the stalk and reducing the wage bill and number of men employed. But why was a young child allowed to climb up on the gove next to a dangerous threshing machine?

> On the 8th, inst., at Bawdsey, on the body of Daniel Girling, aged 3½ years. This little boy and two others were the day before upon the gove in Mr. Bryant's barn, and while Girling's father was throwing down wheat sheaves into a threshing machine, this child slipped down unperceived, and was immediately struck on the head by the wheel of the threshing machine, which killed him on the spot. Verdict "Accidental death."

Another accident involving machinery occurred at Stowupland that month which might well have witnessed one of the first occasions that chloroform was used in Suffolk. Chloroform had been used for the first time as an anaesthetic during a dental procedure in Edinburgh in November 1847 and its use spread rapidly. The accident described here did not cause a sudden death but may have prevented one.

On Friday last as a lad named Isaac Meeking, in the employ of Mr. Edwin Pyman, farmer, of Stowupland, was incautiously playing with a thrashing machine, whilst at work, he got his hand entangled in the machinery, and received so much injury that amputation of the four fingers became necessary. Mr. Clough, from Dr. Freeman's, in company with Dr. Beddingfield, of Stowmarket, performed the operation, and by the aid of chloroform the fingers were taken off and the stumps dressed before the boy was at all conscious that he had been touched, and the hand is going on well.

In February 1848, a determined suicide took place in the parish of Glemsford.

On the 1st February, at Glemsford, on the body of Rachel Skill, housekeeper to Mr. William Mann, of that place, a widow between 40 and 50 years of age, who was that morning found drowned in the mill-pond on Mr. Daniel Peacock's premises. It appeared that the deceased, about nine o'clock the night before, went to the house of Philip Golding, shoemaker, opposite her master's without her bonnet and gave a box and a bundle into the care of Golding's wife, telling her to take particular care of them, and not let anyone but herself or her daughter have them, and left the house quickly, declining to sit down. The box was now produced and found to contain two guineas, two seven shilling pieces, seven sovereigns, two sixpences, and

£45 in banknotes, with two gold rings. The handkerchief contained a dress and lining. Mr. Mann deposed that the deceased had been several years in his service and he had never observed anything particular in her manner. She never said anything about leaving, and appeared pretty comfortable. Nothing could have taken her to the millpond but design to throw herself in; he thought she must have got over the wall to it. Sarah, wife of R. Clarke, of Thorpe, labourer, daughter of the deceased, deposed that her father was a baker in London; her mother came from Fornham St. Martin; she last saw her in the summer, when she told her she did not feel comfortable. The Jury returned a verdict "that the deceased destroyed herself, but as to the state of her mind at the time there is no evidence to satisfy the jurors."

In the same month, sadly, another instance of a child being burnt to death through being left alone for a few minutes by a relative.

At Hartest, on the body of William Webber, aged about four years, who being left by his grandmother whilst she was fetching a pail of water, set fire to his clothes, and was so much burnt that he died after lingering for two weeks. Verdict "Accidental death."

In the May following, another fatal accident resulting in the death of an infant child came about by the careless storage of Lucifer matches.

On the 16th inst., at Martlesham on the body of Arthur Hubbard, whose death was occasioned entirely from the very reprehensible habit of leaving about lucifer matches.

This child was just 2 years old, and being very weak and totally incapable of going alone, was carried every day (since the commencement of the warm weather), into a shed in his father's garden, and placed in a wicker chair there. Some lucifer matches had been carelessly left in the backhouse, and another little boy only six years old, took one into this shed and, rubbing it on a brick, set fire to the shed, which being composed of whins and wood only, and all very dry, blazed up so rapidly that the poor child was suffocated before any person could get to his assistance, and the whole shed soon became a heap of ruins. Had the wind blown in a contrary direction, several cottages would probably have been destroyed. The body of the child presented a shocking appearance from the burning roof having fallen upon him. Verdict "Accidentally burnt." Persons ought to be more careful in keeping lucifers out of the reach of children, who generally think it fine fun to see a blaze.

That same month, a boy drowned in a pond at Framlingham.

On the 12th May, at Framlingham, on the body of Charles Butcher, aged 13 years, son of a labourer, in that parish. Butcher went, with two other boys of his own age, to bathe in a pond, and unconsciously got out of his depth; he was unable to swim, and there being no assistance at hand, nearly an hour elapsed before his body was found. Great praise was awarded to David Pratt and George Smith, two other boys, who could swim, and got Butcher out of the water as soon as they possibly could after hearing that he was in the pond. Verdict "Accidentally drowned."

Yet another child fatality occurred in the cottage home, this time in October 1848 at Middleton, and another sudden death occurred from incautiously riding on the shafts of a heavy waggon.

On Monday last, at Middleton, near Yoxford, on the body of Harry Gardner Watts, aged 2 years and 4 months, son of Mrs. Ellen Blowers. It appeared from the evidence that the child was in the keeping-room with his mother. Whilst her back was turned from him, he went up to the tea-kettle standing on the grate, and sucked the spout. He was so much injured by the steam in the throat, that he died within a few hours, medical assistance having been of no avail. Verdict "Accidental Death."

On Tuesday, at Creeting St. Olave, on the body of Henry Lambert, son of a farmer in that parish aged 46. This was another instance of the incautious habit of riding upon shafts. In returning on Saturday last from Needham Market with his waggon, and whilst standing on the shafts, he put the horses into a gallop, notwithstanding a caution given to him by his brother, Mr. William Lambert, who witnessed the occurrence. He fell from the shafts, when the off fore and hind wheels passed over his head, and killed him on the spot. Verdict "Accidental Death."

In November 1848, a second sudden death and inquest occurred at Middleton.

On Thursday last, at Middleton near Yoxford, on the body of John Smith, aged 19. The deceased, with James Haughley, servants of Mr. R. Garrett, Ironfounder, Leiston, had been entrusted on Monday with the charge of a timber drag, laden with iron, to Peasenhall. After delivering their load, they proceeded to Badingham, where they took up a load of timber, with which they proceeded homewards.

About half past 10 o'clock on Monday night, Mrs. Smith, wife of the gate-keeper of Middleton bar, who was expecting the return of the drag, hearing the sound of horses approaching, went to the door and opened the gate. The horses, however, stopped before reaching it. On going up to the waggon, she found the deceased lying under the wheels, weltering in his blood. She then called to her husband, which awoke Haughley, who was asleep on the load.

Smith was picked up and taken to the gate-house, where he died almost instantly, one of the wheels having passed over his head, and fractured his skull. It appeared also, from the evidence of Haughley, that previously to coming up the hill, about a quarter of a mile from the toll-gate, he asked Smith to drive the load to Theberton. To this Smith agreed, and Haughley then getting on the drag, being very tired, fell asleep. Beyond this, he could give no account of how Smith met with the accident. Verdict "That the deceased died from injuries sustained, but how, or by what means, no direct evidence appeared to the Jurors."

Finally, two sudden deaths and inquest reports from December 1848.

On the 22nd inst., at Wickham Skeith, on the body of Robert Clarke, aged 62 years, who was found dead in the road near Thwaite Buck's Head. It appeared that the deceased had been many years a carpenter in the employ of Mr. Whistlecraft, of Thwaite. Early on the morning of the 20th, the deceased was on his road to work, when he was seized with a fit of apoplexy, and falling on the brow of a ditch, died on the spot. Verdict "Died by the Visitation of God."

On the 26th at Burstall, on the body of Mrs. Hannah Lambert, aged 73, who, on the morning of the 23rd was found dead in her house, with her face against the bars of the grate. It appeared that deceased, who lived alone, whilst sitting close by the fireside, had fallen from her chair in a fit, as no part of her person or clothes was injured except her face, which by the action of the fire was reduced to a cinder, no portion of the features being visible. The jury returned a verdict in accordance with the above facts.

1849 represented another quantitative increase in the occurrence and reporting of sudden deaths in Suffolk. The various ways in which people expired seemed to reach an apotheosis. In January, we read of yet another child's avoidable death.

On the body of William Emmerson, a child of three years old, held at the Three Kings, Fornham All Saints, near Bury St. Edmunds. From the evidence of William Spalding, labourer, and Harriet Emmerson, the sister of the deceased child, it appeared that upon the afternoon of Monday 1st January, the mother left the child with another of more tender years at home, whilst she went to her father's, about 200 yards distant. Upon her return home, and opening the door, she ascertained that smoke filled the chamber, which she entered, and found her child, the eldest, a blackened corpse, fire having caught her clothes, which soon extinguished life. The deceased gave no recognition of life, but merely a slight movement of the arm, which was no doubt in consequence of the excruciating pain it experienced. The mother's shrieks soon brought William Spalding to the scene of woe, but no aid could be given, for life was soon extinct. Mr. Kilner, surgeon, was also present at the termination, but surgical assistance was of no avail.

That same month, a particularly sad case of a man, separated from his wife, who in a depressed state and with a certain amount of forward planning, took his own life. The verdict perhaps did not address the state of mind of the deceased who clearly longed for his wife.

On Saturday, at Henstead, on the body of Mr. William Wilby Carter, farmer of that parish, aged 34, who put an end to his existence by hanging himself in his barn. The circumstances of this case were of a very painful nature. It appeared that the deceased had been separated from his wife, who had left him about three years ago. From the evidence of William Manning, who lived in an adjoining house, it appeared that he saw the deceased on Monday evening the 8th inst., who was then in very low spirits, and had been so for a long time past. The absence of his wife, who had gone to live with her friends, and to whom he was much attached, appeared to be the cause of his depression.

On Tuesday night, about 11 o'clock, when in bed, Manning was called up by the deceased's sister, Miss Carter, who asked Manning to go to look for her brother at a neighbour's house. Not finding the deceased there, Manning returned to the deceased's house, when Miss Carter gave him a note, which he produced, stating that she had found it in deceased's bible. The note was written on a piece of bill paper, and was as follows:- "Let my dear beloved son have my fiddle and squirrel cage; and now I must depart. Read the 16th chapter of St. John, and that will inform you full particulars." At the top of the note was interlined these words, "Give my love to my wife." Manning then made a further search, when he discovered the deceased suspended from a beam in the barn, by a plough line. He was quite cold and stiff, and had been dead some hours.

After a few observations from the Coroner upon the singular selection of the chapter in question, as a reason for such an act, the jury returned a verdict of "Temporary aberration of intellect."

February 1849 saw a spate of suicides around the county.

On Thursday last, at Swilland, on the body of Mr. Frederick Buttram, miller, aged 54, who came by his death under the following melancholy circumstances.

It appeared that shortly after six o'clock that morning, the deceased, who had been suffering for some time under mental derangement, arose from his bed, and unobserved by Mrs. Buttram, dressed himself, and proceeding downstairs, threw himself into a pond adjoining the garden. A labouring man named Knights, about an hour afterwards, in going to the pond for a pail of water, discovered the body.

With the assistance of some neighbours, it was conveyed to the house, but life was extinct. It also appeared that Mr. Acton, surgeon, Grundisburgh, had been in constant attendance upon the deceased for the previous six days, in consequence of the deceased's derangement. The Jury returned a verdict of "Temporary Insanity."

On the 13th inst., at the Half Moon Inn, in the parish of Rattlesden, on the body of George Langham. The following facts were adduced from the examination of several witnesses:- The deceased, a lad of 12 years of age, lived with his aunt, Mrs. Salmon, at Rattlesden. The boy dined with the family, as usual, on the 12th instant, about 1 o'clock, and appeared in his wonted good spirits. Four hours after the lad was missed; a search was instantly made, and after the lapse of an hour, he was found suspended by a halter from a cross beam in a hay-loft over the stable adjoining Mrs. Seggles's house. The body was shortly afterwards cut down, but life was quite extinct.

No reason whatsoever could be ascertained for the wilful deed, deceased being upon that day, and indeed usually, in good spirits; neither was there anything to prey upon his mind, so as to lead him to contemplate suicide. One witness only had once heard him say, about a year ago, that "He would not stop to be beaten, for he would go and hang himself." Verdict by the Jury "Felo de se."

Another case of a child catching fire by the hearth led to a surprising statement of the Jury's feelings in the matter, considering how these deaths were attracting much attention.

On the Feb 23rd, at Benhall, on the body of Charles Goddard, aged 4 years. In the morning of the 10th, his mother left him and a younger child in the house, while she went into the yard for some water. The pump being *out of repair*, it took her nearly five minutes to fill her pail. Before her return to the house, she heard an alarm of fire, and found her child standing at the front door, enveloped in flames, which were quickly extinguished by a kind neighbour, who was also very much burnt. A Surgeon attended the child for several days, but death released him from his sufferings on the 22nd. Verdict "Accidentally burnt." The Jury attached no blame to the mother and the pump has since been repaired.

We should pause for a moment to contemplate the psychological shock that this poor woman suffered at the moment that her child came into view "enveloped in flames." How would she have been affected by this incident for the rest of her life? Her son clung on to life for another twelve days in, what one would assume, would have been intense pain.

A similarly distressing incident came before the Coroner, Mr. S.B. Jackaman, Gent., in Ipswich during April.

Yesterday, at the Angel Inn, St. Clement's, on the body of Jemima Lucock. The deceased was the daughter of a labourer and was between 2 and 3 years of age. On the previous day, about one o'clock, the deceased, unobserved by her mother, drank from the spout of a kettle of boiling water, which was standing on the grate. Mr. Adams, surgeon, was instantly called in, but surgical assistance was of no avail, the poor child dying about 11 at night. Verdict "Accidentally scalded."

There would have been a better chance of survival for the following unfortunate young man but medical assistance was unavailable and so he died.

On the 16th June, at Framlingham, on the body of William Vice, aged 23 years. From the evidence given, it appeared that Vice was found the afternoon before in a small stream of water near the town, and it having been proved that he was subject to violent fits, it is supposed that while in one of such attacks he fell into the water, (with which his body was not covered when found) and he showed signs of life when taken out, though he died in a quarter of an hour. The medical men were all sent for, but not one of them was at home. Verdict, "Accidentally drowned."

The next sudden death in June 1849 occurred almost as the poor woman was entering the churchyard. Perhaps the phrase "Died by the visitation of God" should have been "Died by the visitation TO God."

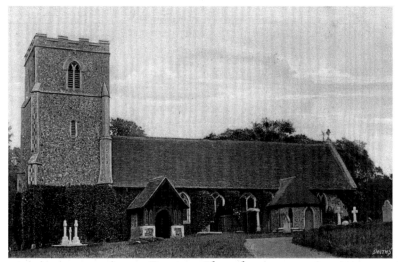
Freston Church

On Monday last, at Freston, on the body of Mrs. Susannah Bradbrook, wife of a respectable farmer in that parish, aged 63. This was a very awful case of sudden death. It appeared that on Sunday morning Mrs. Bradbrook was on her way to church, about a mile distant from her house. Upon entering the churchyard, she suddenly sank down upon the grass, and in a few minutes expired. Immediate assistance was had, and Mr. Cutting, surgeon, sent for, but Mrs. Bradbrook had expired before his arrival.

The deceased was a very stout person, and it is supposed that, apprehensive of being too late for service, she over-exerted herself in walking, and that her death was occasioned by rupture of some vessel of the heart or brain. Verdict "Died by the Visitation of God."

Mr. S.B. Jackaman, Gent., Coroner, was required elsewhere in Ipswich during June when a drowning occurred in the Gipping. Just occasionally, the evidence for a cause of death was not entirely clear cut.

On Wednesday, at the Grey Horse Inn, in the parish of St. Peter, on the body of William Howe, aged two years, when the following evidence was adduced. Harriett Howe, wife of William Howe, shoemaker, residing in the Orchard, of the parish of St. Peter, said the deceased was her son, and that he could walk alone. In the gardens adjoining the river Gipping, the deceased was playing alone that morning about eleven o'clock. Witness was in the house at the time, but the door of the room was open. The garden walk ran straight down to the water.

At the bottom of the garden, there was a fence dividing the garden from the river, but there was no fence at the bottom of the path, although the water was running strongly past at the time. She last saw the deceased playing with a kitten on the walk, and in ten minutes afterwards he was missed. Inquiries were immediately made, and in the course of five minutes, the body of the child was taken out of the river, about 100 yards below the garden. The deceased was an only child, and witness was sure that nobody pushed him into the water.

The next witness called was George Tuck, shoemaker, residing in Gipping Street in the Orchard, who said that about a quarter before eleven, as he was at work, a neighbour called to him saying, "There's a child in the water." He went to the bank when he saw the deceased floating in the middle of the river, on his back, with his clothes distended. The head and face were under, but the mouth and nose out of the water. The spot at which he first saw the deceased was about 50 yards below Howe's garden, where the stream was strong, with a depth of water of about three feet. He took the child out of the river, but observed no signs of life; he thought the deceased bled a little from the nose.

The witness then went on to state that, upon being advised by some ignorant people present, he adopted the reprehensible practice of holding the body up with the head downwards, to let the water run out of the mouth, instead of laying the deceased upon his back, and applying friction, until the arrival of a medical man.

It further appeared from the evidence of Mr. Mills, surgeon, that he arrived promptly, at 11 o'clock, at the house of a Mrs. Tampion, whither the body had been conveyed. For three-quarters of an hour, he applied the usual means to restore animation, but although the body had not been in the water many minutes, life was found to be extinct.

The jury returned the following verdict:- "That the deceased was found drowned and suffocated in the waters of the Gipping; that the said William Howe had no marks of violence on his body; but how or by what means he became drowned or suffocated, no evidence thereof appears to the jurors."

In July 1849, an old lady was found dead in her bedroom. Sometimes the newspaper, by reporting the details of the inquest, stripped the deceased of much of their dignity.

> On Tuesday, at Earl Stonham, on the body of Elizabeth Brame, widow, aged 69. The deceased returned from a visit to her relatives in Essex and London last Sunday, retired to bed at night, and on Monday morning, not having risen at her usual time, one of the neighbours went into her bedroom, and found her dead, the body lying partly on the floor, and partly on the bed; she appeared to have fallen whilst in the act of dressing herself. A report had been circulated that the deceased had died of asiatic cholera, but it clearly appeared that her death proceeded from exhaustion brought on by continued diarrhoea, and the verdict therefore was "Death by natural causes."

During August, presumably whilst Coddenham school was closed for the harvest holiday, an event took place which would have left the inhabitants reeling from the shock of it all. It was reported in the Ipswich Journal as follows:

> An awful occurrence took place on Sunday last, in the village church of Coddenham, to Mr. James Bird, schoolmaster of that parish, who, shortly after entering the church, fell down in a fit of apoplexy, and in a few minutes was a corpse. The sensation caused by this alarming visitation on the congregation may be much better conceived than described. The minister did not proceed with the service, and the parishioners present returned to their homes deeply impressed with the truth of the

declaration, "that in the midst of life, we are in death." The deceased was deservedly respected by his neighbours, and has left a widow and family to lament his loss. He was in his 60th year. An inquest on the body was held on Monday, before J.E. Sparrowe, Esq., when a verdict of "Died by the Visitation of God" was returned.

The circumstances of the following inquest were not uncommon but not always reported in the press.

On Monday last, at Crowfield, on the body of a new born male child, which, on the day before, was found dead in a ditch in that parish. It appeared from the evidence that a young woman, whose name transpired to be Brown, called at the Rose Inn, Crowfield, on Sunday the 26th ult., and asked for a bed. Her appearance at first excited no suspicion. She took tea; but before she retired, the landlady observed that she was pregnant. The woman paid her reckoning, and next morning early decamped, before any of the inmates were astir.

The body was found last Sunday by a boy who was nutting, and was in a very advanced state of decomposition, from having lain in the ditch for a week. The inference was, that the woman Brown was the mother, she having been seen by a boy named Henry Waterman, of whom she asked the way to Helmingham, about a quarter past five on Monday morning, standing in front of the ditch, with a bundle in her arm.

A post mortem examination was made by Mr. Blomfield, surgeon, who stated that from the advanced state of decomposition he could not say whether the child was born alive, or whether any violence had been used. The Coroner summed up the evidence, remarking that no criminal charge would be established against the mother, but that under a recent statute she was liable to punishment for secreting the birth.; when the Jury returned a verdict of "Found dead." She was ordered to be detained by the Rev. J. Bedingfield, who was present at the enquiry, on a charge of secreting the birth.

In October 1849, we learn from inquest reports of terrible tragedies enacted at Needham Market and Melton.

On Wednesday, at Needham Market, on the body of Sarah Marsh, aged 3 years, daughter of William Marsh, labourer. The child came by her death in the following circumstances:- From the evidence of Ann Stevens, a lodger in the house, it appeared that on Wednesday morning, the deceased, with her sister Elizabeth, five years of age, were playing about the bedroom. The mother told them to keep in bed, as she was going out. In 20 minutes, she returned and as soon as she entered the room, she exclaimed, "Good God, my children have been taking poison." Stevens immediately went into the room, when the mother said, "Whatever shall I do? There was some arsenic put on four pieces of bread, which were placed on a basin in a child's chair that was hung up by the side of the wall, so that the children might not reach it." The poison had been laid for the purpose of destroying mice. It further appeared that the husband had been accustomed to put the poisoned bread on the floor during the night, and in the morning to replace it in the chair, to prevent the children having access to it. It happened, however, that the chair containing the poison, was hung over a chest which stood next to the bed, so that the children were able to get on the chest and reach the basin.

By the advice of Mrs. Stevens, the mother took the children immediately to Mr. Pennington, surgeon, who directed the usual remedies to be administered to the youngest, who was soon afterwards taken ill. Mr. Pennington continued his attendance, but the child Sarah died early on Tuesday morning. From the statement of the mother, it appeared that the pieces of bread were each the size of a bean; and that the arsenic had been given to her by a woman named Amos, the quantity placed on the bread not having been more than would have covered a sixpence. The Coroner summed up the evidence, remarking that the case was free from any suspicion of any criminal intention; but that absence of due caution on the part of the parents had led to the event. The jury returned a verdict accordingly.

And at Melton,

On Monday last, at Melton, on the body of Susan Baldry, widow aged 42 years, who hanged herself in the course of the night before. Mrs. Baldry had been in the service of Mr. and Mrs. Sharpe, as housekeeper and lady's maid for more than two years and a half. About a month ago, it was discovered that she had formed a strong attachment to

James Carter, the footman, only 25 years of age. In consequence of which, and for some other cause, Mr. Sharpe on the 13th of September gave Carter notice to quit his service on the 11th of October. Mrs. Baldry immediately became an altered person, low and dejected, and unfit for her daily duties.

On the 28th ult., Mr. Sharpe discharged Carter, at two hours notice, and then Mrs. Baldry became much worse; in fact, so miserable that one of the female servants slept with her every night until the 4th inst., when she said she felt better, and had rather sleep alone. On Monday morning, about 8 o'clock, she was found hanging to the splice of her bed. Mr. Sharpe was called up, who immediately cut her down, but she appeared to have been dead several hours. From his evidence, and that of the two female servants who were examined, the jury were quite satisfied, and returned a verdict of lunacy.

Yet another child death by burning occurred in October 1849. Again the circumstances of the tragedy provoke the questions "How did that happen?" and "What if...?"

Oct 1849: On Saturday, the 29th ult., at Thorpeness, near Aldeburgh, on the body of a child, named Mary Ann Neale, aged three years, the daughter of a labouring man. On the previous Tuesday, the mother went out to make purchases, the deceased with another child in the room, and the father at work in the stable yard. During her absence, which did not exceed ten minutes, the child began to play with the fire and her clothes ignited. The poor thing screamed violently, but the father being stone deaf did not hear her, and when the mother returned, the clothes were nearly burnt off her back. A medical man was sent for, who came and dressed the injured parts, but the child died within two hours. A verdict of "Accidental death" was returned.

A sudden death occurred at the County Gaol in November 1849. A lengthy jail sentence for the rural offender was often almost like a death sentence. Conditions in the jails were awful. Many of those who were released after completing their sentences were too ill to work and they often did not recover.

On Saturday last at the County Gaol, Ipswich, on the body of a prisoner named William Stopher, aged 21, late of Framsden. From the evidence, it appeared that the deceased whilst undergoing an imprisonment of six months for stealing a plough-line, had laboured under occasional attacks of mucous. A few days before his death, he was removed into the infirmary, being at the time labouring under an attack of fever, of which disease, on Saturday morning, he died. The Jury returned a verdict of "Death from typhus fever."

Finally, approaching Christmas 1849, the sad story of a daughter dying almost in her father's arms. This sorrowful event had all the makings of a kitchen sink drama as the doomed girl appeared to have fallen out with her mother-in-law.

On Thursday at Huntingfield, on the body of Lucy Jolly, aged 20, the daughter of Benjamin Jolly, labourer. The deceased, it appeared, had been ailing from tubercular affection of the lungs for several months past. On Saturday last she had a few words with her mother-in-law, in consequence of which she left the house and spent the day with a neighbour. Upon the return of her father from work in the evening, he went to fetch her home, and while returning, her strength suddenly failed, and the father carried her the remainder of the way in his arms. He then sat her down in a chair and in a minute or two afterwards, her head dropped and she expired. It was proved by Mr. Lay, of Peasenhall, that death was purely the result of the before-mentioned disease. Verdict "Died by the Visitation of God."

10

1850 – A Year of Extraordinary Deaths

It has not been the purpose of this book to portray the characters who have had their lives ended suddenly in anything but a sober light. However, even after prolonged studious research on this subject, it is still possible to be shocked, dismayed and even titillated by some of the more bizarre episodes which have been recorded in the newspapers and coroners records. So this final chapter contains some of those bizarre accounts, which leave the reader shaking their head and thinking "Almost unbelievable!"

What better example of a sudden death do we have than the extraordinary suicide carried out in Chediston in January 1850; even more extraordinary when, at the last line, we learn the occupation of the deranged individual......

Before J.E. Sparrowe, Esq., Coroner, on Monday the 7th, at Chediston, near Halesworth, on the body of Edward Etheridge, aged 61 years. The deceased, it seems, had been labouring for some time under a religious hallucination, which manifested itself in a belief that he had no hope of future salvation. The effect of the mind was such as to lead to the rash act of destroying himself, by means of strangling. His body was found by his wife in the hay-chamber of a barn near his house, resting on his knees, with his head in a rope, the other end of which was fastened to a wooden brace against the wall. A verdict of "Temporary Insanity" was returned. It is stated that the deceased is in comfortable circumstances; his occupation was that of a schoolmaster.

A second suicide occurred at Dallinghoo at the same time as the demise of Mr. Etheridge in Chediston. The reporter did not hold back with his description of the incident, the precise detail of which he must have gleaned from the inquest proceedings.

On Wednesday evening last, an inquest was held at Dallinghoo, before John Wood, Esq., Coroner, on the body of Mr. James Elliott, aged 57, of that place. From the evidence, it appeared that the deceased, who was a respectable farmer, had been in a desponding state of mind since the last tithe-feast for the parish, which took place about six weeks ago, and for the last two or three weeks had been in a low and melancholy way. On Wednesday morning, Mr. Elliott got up at his usual hour, and partook of a hearty breakfast, and went out. About eleven o'clock he was found in the meal-house (the key of which the deceased always kept) in a sitting position, upon a low seat, quite dead, with a gun on his right arm, apparently just discharged; a quantity of blood was about his person, and a portion of his brains was lying on the floor of the meal-house. There was a gunshot wound under his right ear and a large part of the left side of his head was blown off. The jury found "That the deceased shot himself with a gun, being at the time of unsound mind."

Suicide was now almost a typical occurrence when farmers were suffering from the agricultural depression of the times and protesting against what were perceived to be unfair tithe rent charges. A number of Suffolk tenant farmers wrote letters to the Ipswich Journal in the early 1850s, directing their ire at their landlords and asking for a reduction in the rates imposed on them. The response was usually negative with the rector or landlord simply pointing out that they were obeying the law with respect to the imposition of the tithe rent charges and were therefore duty-bound to uphold the law.

A third suicide was reported in January, the result of the poverty of a farrier. The details were as follows.

On Saturday last, at the King's Head Inn, Woodbridge, on view of the body of Charles Dunnett, aged 47 years, who hung himself that morning to a beam in the hayloft of the King's Head Inn. From the evidence it appeared that the deceased, who was a horse farrier, had lodged at the King's Head for the last eleven months, and had often complained of poverty to Mr. Cranmer, the landlord, to whom he was indebted, and had for some weeks been in low spirits. It appeared also that deceased who had been attending a horse in the town, was discharged and another farrier called in his place; this, it was supposed, coupled with that of poverty, preyed upon the deceased's mind and led him to the commission of so rash an act.

The deceased was accidentally discovered by Mr. Cranmer hanging in the loft within half an hour after he had been previously seen by him walking up the Market Hill towards his house. He was immediately cut down and bled in the neck by two surgeons, who were instantly in attendance, but to no avail, and was pronounced quite dead. The deceased was a single man and was found without any money whatever on his person. Verdict: "That the deceased destroyed himself whilst labouring under temporary insanity."

Towards the end of the month of January, three more reports of sudden deaths caught the eye, giving the reader some further indication of the social mores amongst the labouring classes in the middle of the 19th century.

A most melancholy accident occurred on Thursday afternoon in this town (Eye). Two men in the employ of Mr. Read, of Wortham, were returning home in a state of intoxication, with a waggon load of iron hurdles, when they both fell in front of the wheels, which passed over their bodies, and they were killed on the spot. Surely this ought to be a caution to farmers not to trust drunkards with their horses.

On the 29th at Gedding, on the body of Caroline, daughter of Samuel Pilbrow, mole-catcher, aged three years, who was seized with sickness and purging, and died within a few hours. Mr. White, from a post-mortem examination, considered death to have been caused by an attack of English cholera; but "presenting the features of many which have been returned as Asiatic cholera." It further appeared that all Pilbrow's children had been attacked in a similar manner about a month or six weeks previous; and that at the back of the house, about two or three yards off the door, is a ditch into which the privies of cottages occupied by upwards of 30 people are emptied. It is quite open and offensive. The property belongs to Mr. Wm. Wade who lives in one of the cottages. Verdict, "Natural Death."

On Monday last, whilst a girl named Eliza Cook, aged 12 years, and living at Lambert's Buildings, Risbygate Street, in this town, was dressing her infant brother adjacent to the fireplace, her clothes caught fire and were immediately in a blaze. A neighbour ran in upon hearing an outcry, and finding the girl enveloped in flames, proceeded to extinguish the fire by throwing water upon the sufferer, which had the desired effect. She was then removed to bed, attended by a surgeon, but to no avail, as within ten hours she breathed her last. Her sufferings were so severe and of so awful a character, that the party who held her during these agonising moments, avowed that the skin and a portion of the flesh, where the hands were placed, were detached from the body. An inquest was held and the jury returned a verdict of "Accidental Death."

This was a frantic start to the year for the coroners with all manner of sudden deaths having to be dealt with and they having to travel from parish to parish in difficult weather conditions.

On Saturday 9th Feb., at Henham, on the body of Edward Burton, aged 14 years. The deceased was in the employ of the Earl of Stradbroke, on the Park Farm, Henham. On Wednesday 6th, during the prevalence of the storm of wind, he was holding a gate open for a fellow labourer to pass through, when a gust of wind threw the gate against him, which forced him down, and inflicted a blow on the vertebrae of the neck, causing instant death. Verdict, "Accidental death."

Before Mr. S.B. Jackaman, Gent., Coroner, on February 15th, on the body of Henry Ludbrook, aged 7 years. The deceased child, it appeared, was on the Quays by the Wet Dock, picking up pieces of coal which fall from the railway trucks whilst being loaded (a common practice, by all accounts) when he was crushed between the buffers of two trucks on the tramway. The death of the deceased was proved to be entirely accidental and the Jury returned a verdict accordingly. "The Jury unanimously desired to represent to the Dock Commissioners that measures should be taken, without delay, to prevent children frequenting the Dock Quays, for the purpose of picking up coal or grain, and appropriating the same for the use of their parents or friends, whereby the lives and morals of the children were alike endangered."

The Coroner for the Liberty and Borough of Bury St. Edmunds, Harry Wayman, Esq., was also kept busy in February 1850.

On the 13th inst., at Lawshall, on the body of George Billerman, about 24 years of age, who on his return from Glemsford to Mr. Smith's farm at Hawstead, with a four-horse waggon laden with turnips, was running by the side of the shaft-horse as they trotted down Coldham Hill, when he fell, and both the near wheels went over the upper part of his body and he was killed on the spot. The deceased had been drinking at Hartest, and in the opinion of John Cook, who was riding on the shafts at the time, it was owing to his being "fresh" that he fell down. Verdict: "Accidental death."

On the 19th inst., at the White Hart, Tuddenham, upon the body of Philip Rumbelow, master blacksmith. From the evidence adduced, it appeared that the deceased was missed on Monday, the 18th; a search was made and after the lapse of some time, he was found in a stable adjoining his own premises, lying on the ground upon his back, with a razor beside him, his hand besmeared with blood, and throat cut - the windpipe being entirely severed. Deceased had for some days previous exhibited great lowness of spirits, for which there was no apparent cause, he having a large and prosperous business. Deceased was 53 years of age. The Jury returned a verdict of "Temporary Derangement."

Two dreadful accidents involving farm machinery occurred in April. In the first, the child survived but in the second accident the labourer eventually succumbed to the massive loss of blood that he suffered.

On Saturday, a boy named Walter Smith, aged 8 years, son of a labourer of that name residing in the parish of St. Clement, Ipswich, met with a most deplorable accident. It appears that, accompanied by a younger brother, he had strayed to the premises of a neighbour when they commenced playing with a chaff-engine. After turning the wheel, it was found to have acquired too much impetus. Whilst endeavouring to stop it, the boy missed the handle, when his arm got between the knives and the result was that his left hand was severed from the arm just below the wrist.

He was conveyed to the hospital, when it was found necessary again to amputate higher up the arm, and we are glad to say the poor child is now doing well.

On Wednesday, as William Green, labourer, in the employ of Lady Harland at the Wherstead farm, was engaged with a horse-power chaff engine, his leg becoming entangled with the wheel was severely lacerated. He was promptly removed to the Hospital, where it was discovered that one of the principal arteries had been divided. The poor fellow was much exhausted from haemorrhage.

For the next occurrence of sudden death, we return to the Liberty of Bury St. Edmunds, and Coroner Mr. Harry Wayman, Esq., who dealt with the following shocking event in May.

On the 3rd inst., at Ixworth, on the body of Hannah Claxton, aged 10, who being left in the care of the house while the mother went to Pakenham, lighted a fire to dry the baby's clothes, and by some means set her own clothes on fire. She had at the time an infant in her arms, and rushed into the street, where two women succeeded in putting out the fire and in rescuing the baby, whose clothes were partly burnt. The deceased sustained such severe injuries as to cause her death after several days of suffering. Verdict, "Accidental Death."

Goodness knows what the poor mother must have thought when she came back from Pakenham. This story did not end there. The baby, Jane Claxton, died two years later. The family were already without their father, James, who had died in 1849. The mother

Eliza and her two remaining young children, Mary Ann and William, faced the prospect of a life of abject poverty. Eliza had little choice but to re-marry which she did to William Lambert, a labourer, in 1853. There would then have been at least one bread-winner in the household.

The Greyhound Inn, Ixworth

Once again we learn more of the desperate lives of some of the poor labouring families in mid-19th century Suffolk.

Another 10 year old died during the month of May - this sudden death concerned a boy who was in charge of a massive horse and a tumbril of manure - a practise that surely should never have been allowed to happen (but inevitably did).

On the 21st inst., at Alderton, on view of the body of Edward Read, aged 10 years. It appears from the evidence that the deceased was, on the 15th, carting manure with a one horse tumbril, and contrary to a previous caution from his fellow servants, got upon the horse he was driving, and from a statement made by him previous to his death, it would seem the horse kicked, threw him off, and ran away, leaving this poor boy in the road, where he was picked up; one of the wheels having passed over the lower part of his body it caused a rupture, of which he lingered in great pain until the 20th, when he died. Verdict, "Accidental Death."

Alderton High Street

In the month of July, a very afflicting case of accidental poisoning came up for investigation before Mr. S.B. Jackaman, Esq., Coroner. The inquest was held at the Steam Packet Inn, in the parish of St. Clement, the deceased, Alfred 3 years of age, being the son of Mr. H.W. Girling, a hatter.

From the testimony of the witnesses, it appeared that for the last month, the health of the child, from the effects of a cough, had been very indifferent. On Friday night, his mother made a cough mixture, the ingredients being a pennyworth of laudanum, half a pound of treacle and a quarter of vinegar. A small teaspoonful was administered three times daily and the child became relieved.

On Tuesday morning, about six o'clock, after passing a bad night, the child fell asleep. The bottle containing the mixture stood on a chest of drawers in the bedroom. About nine, the child came downstairs, with his clothes under his arm, to be dressed, saying, "I'm a good boy, I've taken all my cough mixture." The mother instantly became alarmed and found that the deceased had taken the rest of the mixture, as much as would fill two wine glasses, leaving nothing but the empty bottle. At 11 o'clock, he became stupid, with an affection of the eyes. Some castor oil and other simple remedies were administered, and the child fell asleep. At two o'clock he awoke, frothing at the mouth, and discharging from the nose a thick yellow matter.

Dr. Royle was promptly in attendance. He found the functions of the brain nearly superseded; the surface of the body cold; and the patient nearly pulseless. He was at once convinced that the child had taken some strong narcotic poison; and notwithstanding the application of every known remedy, the patient died the same night at eight.

In the opinion of Dr. Royle, two wine glasses of the mixture were quite sufficient to produce death, containing, as they had done, a grain of opium; and that death was caused by congestion of the brain. Dr. Royle added that the mixture in question was a very popular remedy for a cough, but that it behoved mothers and nurses to administer it with great judgement and discrimination. The jury returned the following verdict: "That the deceased died from congestion of the brain, occasioned by accidentally taking two glasses of cough mixture, compounded by his mother, and containing laudanum."

Crabbing at Walberswick is a very popular modern-day pursuit of parents and their young children and it was also popular in the district in 1850, although the dangers to very young children were probably not well understood. Consequently, a fatality was always likely to happen and did happen in Blythburgh in July.

On Monday last, at Blythburgh, on view of the body of Charles Etheridge, aged 5 years. He and several other children were playing on the bank of the river near the bridge, dabbing for crabs. The little urchins were warned of their danger, but they replied, "Oh, if we do fall in, we can swim." No sooner was this warning pronounced than the deceased fell in, and was carried down by the tide below the bridge, when he was picked up by some people engaged in hay making in an adjoining field. Means were taken to restore animation, but without effect. The Jury returned a verdict of "Accidental Death."

We move on to early September for the next sudden death, which was unusual not for the manner in which death struck the individual, but in the curious circumstances by which the inquest had to take place - in the church vestry.

> Before G.A. Partridge, Gent., Deputy Coroner for the Liberty and Borough of Bury St. Edmunds. On the 5th inst. at Westley, on the body of Charles Nunn, in the employ of Mr. G. Steward, of Hargrave, who whilst sitting on the fore part of a waggon, fell off and the wheel, passing over his body, killed him on the spot. A verdict of "Accidental death" was returned. On the arrival of the Coroner, the body was found lying in the church porch, the custom, it appears in the parish, and there being no public house in which the inquest could be held, the Jury assembled in the vestry.

The final three reports in November 1850 return us to the principal causes of sudden deaths in Suffolk that we have read about, namely deaths involving agricultural equipment and child deaths by burning.

> On the 4th inst., at Benhall, on the body of Solomon Cook, aged 3½ years, who was burnt to death early the preceding morning, in the temporary absence of his mother. It is rather remarkable that this woman lost another child by similar means, in the same parish, about 8 years before. The jury were, therefore, more stringent in their enquiries; but being quite satisfied that the death of this child was also the result of accident, unanimously agreed in a verdict to that effect.

> On Tuesday, at Walpole, near Halesworth, on view of the body of William Atkins, aged 16. The deceased was the son-

in-law of Mr. James Smith, farmer, of that parish. On the 2nd inst., he was engaged in a field adjoining the house, in guiding a two-horse roll. Whilst turning the horses, he suddenly fell across the roll, one end of which rested upon the back of his head, whereby he was pressed into the earth and suffocated. When taken up immediately afterwards, he was found dead. Verdict, "Accidental Death."

On the 18th inst., at Groton, on the body of Charles Gant, aged 12, who, being in the employ of Mr. Strutt, was driving an empty muck cart with two young horses, when they started off, and, knocking him down, the wheel went over the lower part of his body and inflicted such injuries as to cause his death the same day. Verdict, "Accidental Death."

Boxford White Hart (once listed as being in Groton)

In the cases of the young boys who were the victims of fatal injury involving farm machinery, one wonders how it was that teenage boys could be allocated such work involving heavy machinery and large horses. Sadly, the young boys of poor labouring families had to find work at an early age to supplement the meagre family income. Their education was secondary to their usefulness earning a couple of shillings a week. It would be at least another quarter of a century before legislation was enacted which would make school attendance compulsory and raise the school leaving age above 12 years.

The significance of Solomon Cook's death is that the mother repeated the mistake of leaving her child unattended, as she had done in 1842 when her infant daughter Mary Ann was also burnt to death. It would not be a harsh verdict to describe the mother as being culpable for her son's death.

And yet in the Coroners Courts of the period covered by this book, these accidents were considered by the local juries as unfortunate tragedies. The Coroner had no legal power to send a neglectful mother for prosecution. It was the jury of local men that came to a verdict and almost invariably offered no further comment on the causes of the death. The leniency of the juries and the complete inadequacy of existing laws meant that very little attention was paid to those continuing family tragedies, which were occurring in the centre of family life around the unprotected hearth.

It would not be until the 1870s that the Government would enact the first general legislation aimed at protecting the welfare of infants. Specific legislation regarding children and fireguards in the home would only be enacted with the passing of the Children Act in 1908. Until then, the deaths of young children from burning in the family home were not legislated for and therefore the incidence of such tragedies continued unabated. The story of how this legislation was developed amidst an increasingly industrialised society is a story for another to tell.

It is to be hoped that the reader has gained an impression from the examples in this book on how vulnerable the poor of Suffolk were to the hazards of everyday life in the first half of the 19th century and that it was not just disease that carried off the unfortunate soul "by the Visitation of God."

Index of Parishes